STUDY GUIDE

The Tragedy of Hamlet

William Shakespeare

WITH CONNECTIONS

HOLT, RINEHART AND **WINSTON**
Harcourt Brace & Company
Austin • New York • Orlando • Atlanta • San Francisco • Boston • Dallas • Toronto • London

Staff Credits

Director: Mescal Evler

Manager of Editorial Operations: Bill Wahlgren

Executive Editor: Katie Vignery

Book Editor: Carolyn Logan

Editorial Staff: *Managing Editor,* Marie Price; *Copyediting Manager,* Michael Neibergall; *Copyediting Supervisor,* Abigail Winograd; *Senior Copyeditors,* Susan Kent Cakars, John Haffner Layden, Leora Harris, Mary Malone; *Copyeditors,* Joel Bourgeois, Julie Byre, Ed Cohen, Gabrielle Field, Suzi A. Hunn, Jane Kominek, Lanie Lee, Millicent Ondras, Theresa Reding, Désirée Reid, Kathleen Scheiner; *Editorial Operations Coordinator,* Lori De La Garza; *Editorial Coordinators,* Heather Cheyne, Mark Holland, Marcus Johnson, Jill O'Neal, Janet Riley; *Word Processors,* Ruth Hooker, Margaret Sanchez, Liz Dickson, Gail Coupland

Permissions: Lee Noble, Catherine Paré

Design: *Design Director,* Joe Melomo; *Art Buyer Supervisor,* Elaine Tate

Prepress Production: Beth Prevelige, Simira Davis, Joan Lindsay

Manufacturing Coordinator: Michael Roche

Electronic Publishing: *Operators,* JoAnn Brown, Lana Knapp, Indira Konanur, Christopher Lucas, Nanda Patel; *Administrative Coordinator,* Sally Williams

TABLE *of* CONTENTS

TABLE *of* CONTENTS

Using This Study Guide

Approaching the Play

The successful study of a play often depends on students' enthusiasm, curiosity, and openness. The ideas in **Introducing the Play** will help you create such a climate for your class. Background information in **Focusing on Background** and **About the Play** can also be used to pique students' interest.

Guided Reading questions are designed to help students interpret the play as they read it.

Reading and Responding to the Play

Making Meanings questions are designed for both individual response and group or class discussion. They range from personal response to high-level critical thinking.

Reading Strategies worksheets contain graphic organizers. They help students explore techniques that enhance both comprehension and literary analysis. Many worksheets are appropriate for more than one set of chapters.

Play Notes provide high-interest information relating to historical, cultural, literary, and other elements of the play. The **Investigate** questions and **Reader's Log** ideas guide students to further research and consideration.

Choices suggest a wide variety of activities for exploring different aspects of the play, either individually or collaboratively. The results may be included in a portfolio or used as springboards for larger projects.

Vocabulary Worksheets consist of exercises using words from the play.

Reader's Log, Double-Entry Journal, and **Group Discussion Log** model formats and spark ideas for responding to the play. These pages are designed to be a resource for independent reading as well.

Responding to the Play as a Whole

The following features provide options for culminating activities that can be used in whole-class, small-group, or independent-study situations.

Play Review provides a format for summarizing and integrating the major literary elements.

Play Projects suggest multiple options for culminating activities. **Writing About the Play, Cross-Curricular Connections,** and **Multimedia and Internet Connections** propose project options that extend the text into other genres, content areas, and environments.

Responding to the Connections

Making Meanings questions in **Exploring the Connections** facilitate discussion of the additional readings in the HRW LIBRARY edition of this play.

This Study Guide is intended to

- *provide maximum versatility and flexibility*
- *serve as a ready resource for background information on both the playwright and the play*
- *act as a catalyst for discussion, analysis, interpretation, activities, and further research*
- *provide reproducible masters that can be used for either individual or collaborative work, including discussions and projects*
- *provide multiple options for evaluating students' progress through the play and the Connections*

Literary Elements

- plot structure
- major themes
- characterization
- setting
- point of view
- symbolism, irony, and other elements appropriate to the title

Making Meanings Reproducible Masters

- First Thoughts
- Shaping Interpretations
- Connecting with the Text
- Extending the Text
- Challenging the Text

A **Reading Check** focuses on review and comprehension.

The Worksheets Reproducible Masters

- Reading Strategies Worksheets
- Literary Elements Worksheets
- Vocabulary Worksheets

Reaching All Students

Because the questions and activities in this Study Guide are in the form of reproducible masters, labels indicating the targeted types of learners have been omitted.

Strategies for inclusion provides ideas for modifying instruction to suit the needs of individuals students.

Most classrooms include students from a variety of backgrounds and with a range of learning styles. The questions and activities in this Study Guide have been developed to meet diverse student interests, abilities, and learning styles. Of course, students are full of surprises, and a question or activity that is challenging to an advanced student can also be handled successfully by students who are less proficient readers. The interest level, flexibility, and variety of these questions and activities make them appropriate for a range of students.

Struggling Readers and Students with Limited English Proficiency: The **Making Meanings** questions, the **Choices** activities, and the **Reading Strategies** worksheets all provide opportunities for students to check their understanding of the text and to review their reading. The **Play Projects** ideas are designed for a range of student abilities and learning styles. Both questions and activities motivate and encourage students to make connections to their own interests and experiences. The **Vocabulary Worksheets** can be used to facilitate language acquisition. **Dialogue Journals,** with you the teacher or with more advanced students as respondents, can be especially helpful to these students.

Advanced Students: The writing opportunity suggested with the **Making Meanings** questions and the additional research suggestions in **Play Notes** should offer a challenge to these students. The **Choices** and **Play Projects** activities can be taken to advanced levels. **Dialogue Journals** allow advanced students to act as mentors or to engage each other intellectually.

Auditory Learners: A range of suggestions in this Study Guide targets students who respond particularly well to auditory stimuli: making and listening to audiotapes and engaging in class discussion, role-playing, debate, oral reading, and oral presentation. See **Making Meanings** questions, **Choices,** and **Play Projects** options (especially **Cross-Curricular Connections** and **Multimedia and Internet Connections**).

Visual/Spatial Learners: Students are guided to create visual representations of play scenes and concepts and to analyze films or videos in **Choices** and in **Play Projects.** The **Reading Strategies** and **Literary Elements Worksheets** utilize graphic organizers as a way to both assimilate and express information.

Tactile/Kinesthetic Learners: The numerous interactive, hands-on, and problem-solving projects are designed to encourage the involvement of students motivated by action and movement. The projects also provide an opportunity for **interpersonal learners** to connect with others through play-related tasks. The **Group Discussion Log** will help students track the significant points of their interactions.

Verbal Learners: For students who naturally connect to the written and spoken word, the **Reader's Logs** and **Dialogue Journals** will have particular appeal. This Study Guide offers numerous writing opportunities: See **Making Meanings, Choices, Play Notes,** and **Writing About the Play** in **Play Projects.** These options should also be attractive to **intrapersonal learners.**

Assessment Options

Perhaps the most important goal of assessment is to provide feedback on the effectiveness of instructional strategies. As you monitor the degree to which your students understand and engage with the play, you will naturally adjust the frequency and ratio of class to small-group and verbal to nonverbal activities, as well as the extent to which direct teaching of reading strategies, literary elements, or vocabulary is appropriate to your students' needs.

If you are in an environment where **portfolios** contain only carefully chosen samples of students' writing, you may want to introduce a second, "working," portfolio and negotiate grades with students after examining all or selected items from this portfolio.

The features in this Study Guide are designed to facilitate a variety of assessment techniques.

Reader's Logs and Double-Entry Journals can be briefly reviewed and responded to (students may wish to indicate entries they would prefer to keep private). The logs and journals are an excellent measure of students' engagement with and understanding of the play.

Group Discussion Log entries provide students with an opportunity for self-evaluation of their participation in both book discussions and project planning.

Making Meanings questions allow you to observe and evaluate a range of student responses. Those who have difficulty with literal and interpretive questions may respond more completely to **Connecting** and **Extending**. The **Writing Opportunity** provides you with the option of ongoing assessment: You can provide feedback to students' brief written responses to these prompts as they progress through the play.

Reading Strategies Worksheets, Play Review, and Literary Elements Worksheets lend themselves well to both quick assessment and students' self-evaluation. They can be completed collaboratively and the results shared with the class, or students can compare their individual responses in a small-group environment.

Choices activities and writing prompts offer all students the chance to successfully complete an activity, either individually or collaboratively, and share the results with the class. These items are ideal for peer evaluation and can help prepare students for presenting and evaluating larger projects at the completion of the play unit.

Vocabulary Worksheets can be used as diagnostic tools or as part of a concluding test.

Play Projects evaluations might be based on the degree of understanding of the play demonstrated by the project. Students' presentations of their projects should be taken into account, and both self-evaluation and peer evaluation can enter into the overall assessment.

The final **Test** and the tests for each act are traditional assessment tools in three parts: objective items, short-answer questions, and essay questions.

Questions for Self-evaluation and Goal Setting

- What are the three most important things I learned in my work with this play?
- How will I follow up so that I remember them?
- What was the most difficult part of working with this play?
- How did I deal with the difficulty, and what would I do differently?
- What two goals will I work toward in my reading, writing, group, and other work?
- What steps will I take to achieve those goals?

Items for a "Working" Portfolio

- reading records
- drafts of written work and project plans
- audio- and videotapes of presentations
- notes on discussions
- reminders of cooperative projects, such as planning and discussion notes
- artwork
- objects and mementos connected with themes and topics in the play
- other evidence of engagement with the play

For help with establishing and maintaining portfolio assessment, examine the **Portfolio Management System** *in* ELEMENTS OF LITERATURE.

Answer Key

The Answer Key at the back of this guide is not intended to be definitive or to set up a right-wrong dichotomy. In questions that involve interpretation, however, students' responses should be defended by citations from the text.

The Life and Work of William Shakespeare (1564–1616) by C. F. Main

C. F. Main was for many years a professor of English at Rutgers University in New Brunswick, New Jersey. He is the editor of Poems: Wadsworth Handbook and Anthology *and has written reviews and articles on sixteenth-, seventeenth-, and eighteenth-century literature.*

Every literate person has heard of William Shakespeare, the author of more than three dozen remarkable plays and more than 150 poems. Over the centuries, these literary works have made such a deep impression on the human race that all sorts of fancies, legends, and theories have been invented about their author. There are even those who say that somebody other than Shakespeare wrote the works that bear his name, although these deluded people cannot agree on who, among a dozen candidates, this other author actually was. Such speculation is based on the wrong assumption that little is known about Shakespeare's life; in fact, Shakespeare's life is better documented than the life of any other dramatist of the time except perhaps Ben Jonson, a writer who seems almost modern in the way he publicized himself. Jonson was an honest, blunt, and outspoken man who knew Shakespeare well; for a time the two dramatists wrote for the same theatrical company, and Shakespeare even acted in Jonson's plays. Often stingy in his praise of other writers, Jonson published a poem asserting that Shakespeare was superior to all Greek, Roman, and English dramatists and predicting that he would be "not of an age, but for all time." Jonson's judgment is now commonly accepted, and his prophecy has come true.

Shakespeare was born in Stratford-on-Avon, a historic and prosperous market town in Warwickshire, and was christened in the parish church there on April 26, 1564. His father was John Shakespeare, a merchant at one time active in the town government; his mother—born Mary Arden—came from a prominent family in the country. For seven years or so, William attended the Stratford Grammar School, where he obtained an excellent education in Latin, the Bible, and English composition. (The students had to write out English translations of Latin words and then turn them back into Latin.) After leaving school, he may have been apprenticed to a butcher, but because he shows in his plays very detailed knowledge of many different crafts and trades, scholars have proposed a number of different occupations that he could have followed. At eighteen, Shakespeare married Anne Hathaway, the twenty-seven-year-old daughter of a farmer living near Stratford. They had three children, a daughter named Susanna and a pair of twins named Hamnet and Judith. We don't know how the young Shakespeare supported his family, but according to tradition he taught school for a few years. The two daughters grew up and married; the son died when he was eleven.

How did Shakespeare first become interested in the theater? Presumably by seeing plays. We know that traveling acting companies frequently visited Stratford, and we assume that he attended their performances and that he also went to the nearby city of Coventry where a famous cycle of religious plays was put on every year. But to be a dramatist, one had to be in London, where the theater was flourishing in the 1580s. Just when Shakespeare left his family and moved to London (there is no evidence that his wife was ever in the city) is uncertain; scholars say that he arrived there in 1587 or 1588. It is certain that he was busy and successful in the London theater by 1592, when a fellow dramatist named Robert Greene attacked him in print and ridiculed a passage in his early play *Henry VI*. Greene, a down-and-out Cambridge graduate, warned other university men then writing plays to beware of this "upstart crow beautified with our feathers." Green died of dissipation just as his ill-natured attack was being published, but a friend of his named Henry Chettle immediately apologized in print to Shakespeare and commended Shakespeare's acting and writing ability, and his personal honesty.

From 1592 on there is ample documentation of Shakespeare's life and works. We know where he lived in London, at least approximately when his plays were produced and printed, and even how he spent his money. From 1594 to his retirement in about 1613, he was continuously a member of one company, which also included the great tragic actor Richard Burbage and the popular clown Will Kemp. Although actors and others connected with the theater had a very low status legally, in practice they enjoyed the patronage of noblemen and even royalty. It is a mistake to think of Shakespeare as an obscure actor who somehow wrote great plays; he was well known even as a young man. He first became famous as the author of a best-seller, an erotic narrative poem called *Venus and Adonis* (1593). This poem, as well as a more serious one entitled *The Rape of Lucrece* (1594), was dedicated to a rich and extravagant young nobleman, the Earl of Southampton. The dedication of *The Rape of Lucrece* suggests that Shakespeare and his patron were on very friendly terms.

Shakespeare's Early Plays

Among Shakespeare's earliest plays are the following, with the generally but not universally accepted dates of their first performance: *Richard III* (1592–1593), a "chronicle" or history play about a deformed usurper who became king of England; *The Comedy of Errors* (1592–1594), a rowdy farce of mistaken identity based on a Latin play; *Titus Andronicus* (1593–1594), a blood-and-thunder tragedy full of rant and atrocities; *The Taming of the Shrew, The Two Gentlemen of Verona,* and *Love's Labor's Lost* (all 1593–1595), three agreeable comedies; and *Romeo and Juliet*

(1595–1596), a poetic tragedy of ill-fated lovers. The extraordinary thing about these plays is not so much their immense variety—each one is quite different from all the others—but the fact that they are all regularly revived and performed on stages all over the world today.

By 1596 Shakespeare was beginning to prosper. He had his father apply to the Heralds' College for a coat of arms that the family could display, signifying that they were "gentlefolks." On Shakespeare's family crest a falcon is shown, shaking a spear. To support this claim to gentility, Shakespeare bought New Place, a handsome house and grounds in Stratford, a place so commodious and elegant that the queen of England once stayed there after Shakespeare's daughter Susanna inherited it. Shakespeare also, in 1599, joined with a few other members of his company, now called the Lord Chamberlain's Men, to finance a new theater on the south side of the Thames—the famous Globe. The "honey-tongued Shakespeare," as he was called in a book about English literature published in 1598, was now earning money as a playwright, an actor, and a shareholder in a theater. By 1600, Shakespeare was regularly associating with members of the aristocracy, and six of his plays had been given command performances at the court of Queen Elizabeth.

During the last years of Elizabeth I's reign, Shakespeare completed his cycle of plays about England during the Wars of the Roses: *Richard II* (1595), both parts of *Henry IV* (1596–1598), and *Henry V* (1599). Also in this period he wrote the play most frequently studied in schools—*Julius Caesar* (1599)—and the comedies that are most frequently performed today: *A Midsummer Night's Dream* (1595–1596), *The Merchant of Venice* (1596–1597), *Much Ado About Nothing* (1598–1599), and *As You Like It* and *Twelfth Night* (1599–1600). And finally at this time he wrote or rewrote *Hamlet* (1600–1601), the tragedy that, of all his tragedies, has provoked the most varied and controversial interpretations from critics, scholars, and actors.

Shakespeare indeed prospered under Queen Elizabeth; according to an old tradition, she asked him to write *The Merry Wives of Windsor* (1597) because she wanted to see the merry, fat old knight Sir John Falstaff (of the *Henry* plays) in love.

He prospered even more under Elizabeth's successor, King James of Scotland. Fortunately for Shakespeare's company, as it turned out, James's royal entry into London in 1603 had to be postponed for several months because the plague was raging in the city. While waiting for the epidemic to subside, the royal court stayed in various palaces outside London. Shakespeare's company took advantage of this situation and, since the city theaters were closed, performed several plays for the court and the new king. Shakespeare's plays delighted James, for he loved literature and was starved for pleasure after the grim experience of ruling Scotland for many years. He immediately took the company under his patronage, renamed them the King's Men, gave them patents to perform anywhere in the realm, provided them with special clothing for state occasions, increased their salaries, and appointed their chief members, including Shakespeare, to be Grooms of the Royal Chamber. All this patronage brought such prosperity to Shakespeare that he was able to make some very profitable real estate investments in Stratford and London.

Shakespeare's "Tragic Period"

In the early years of the seventeenth century, while his financial affairs were flourishing and everything was apparently going very well for Shakespeare, he wrote his greatest tragedies: *Hamlet* (already mentioned), *Othello* (1604), *King Lear* (1605), *Macbeth* (1606), and *Antony and Cleopatra* (1606–1607). Because these famous plays are so preoccupied with evil, violence, and death, some people feel that Shakespeare must have been very unhappy and depressed when he wrote them. Moreover, such people find even the comedies he wrote at this time more sour than sweet: *Troilus and*

Cressida (1601–1602), *All's Well That Ends Well* (1602–1603), and *Measure for Measure* (1604). And so, instead of paying tribute to Shakespeare's powerful imagination, which is everywhere evident, these people invent a "tragic period" in Shakespeare's biography, and they search for personal crises in his private life. When they cannot find these agonies, they invent them. To be sure, in 1607 an actor named Edward Shakespeare, who may well have been William's younger brother, died in London. But by 1607 Shakespeare's alleged "tragic period" was almost over!

It is quite wrong to assume a one-to-one correspondence between writers' lives and their works because writers must be allowed to imagine whatever they can. It is especially wrong in the case of a writer like Shakespeare, who did not write to express himself but to satisfy the patrons of the theater that he and his partners owned. Shakespeare must have repeatedly given the audience just what it wanted; otherwise, he could not have made so much money out of the theater. To insist that he had to experience and feel personally everything that he wrote about is absurd. He wrote about King Lear, who cursed his two monstrous daughters for treating him very badly; in contrast, what evidence there is suggests that he got along very well with his own two daughters. And so, instead of "tragic," we should think of the years 1600–1607 as glorious, because in them Shakespeare's productivity was at its peak. It seems very doubtful that a depressed person would write plays like these. In fact, they would make their creator feel exhilarated rather than sad.

The Last Years

In 1612 Shakespeare decided that, having made a considerable sum from his plays and theatrical enterprises, he would retire to his handsome house in Stratford, a place he had never forgotten, though he seems to have kept his life there rather separate from his life in London. His retirement was not complete, for the records show that after he returned to Stratford, he still took part in the management of the King's Men and their two theaters: the Globe, a polygonal building opened in 1599 and used for performances in good weather, and the Blackfriars, acquired in 1608 and used for indoor performances. Shakespeare's works in this period show no signs of diminished creativity, except that in some years he wrote one play instead of the customary two, and they continue to illustrate the great diversity of his genius. Among them are the tragedies *Timon of Athens* (1607–1608) and *Coriolanus* (1607–1608) and five plays that have been variously classified as comedies, romances, or tragicomedies: *Pericles* (1607–1608), *Cymbeline* (1609–1610), *The Winter's Tale* (1610–1611), *The Tempest* (1611), and *The Two Noble Kinsmen* (1613). His last English history play, *Henry VIII* (1612–1613), contains a tribute to Queen Elizabeth—a somewhat tardy tribute, because, unlike most of the other poets of the day, Shakespeare did not praise her in print when she died in 1603. (Some scholars argue, on very little evidence, that he was an admirer of the Earl of Essex, a former intimate of Elizabeth's whom she had beheaded for rebelliousness.) During the first performance of *Henry VIII*, in June of 1613, the firing of the cannon at the end of Act I set the Globe on fire (it had a thatched roof), and it burned to the ground. Only one casualty is recorded: A bottle of ale had to be poured on a man whose breeches were burning. Fortunately, the company had the Blackfriars in which to perform until the Globe could be rebuilt and reopened in 1614.

Shakespeare's last recorded visit to London, accompanied by his son-in-law Dr. John Hall, was in November 1614, though he may have gone down to the city afterward because he continued to own property there, including a building very near the Blackfriars Theater. Probably, though, he spent most of the last two years of his life at New Place, with his daughter Susanna Hall (and his granddaughter Elizabeth) living nearby. He died on April 23, 1616,

and was buried under the floor of Stratford Church, with this epitaph warning posterity not to dig him up and transfer him to the graveyard outside the church—a common practice in those days when space was needed:

> Good friend, for Jesus' sake forbear
> To dig the dust enclosèd here!
> Blest be the man that spares these stones,
> And curst be he that moves my bones.

Shakespeare's Genius

What sort of man was Shakespeare? This is a hard question to answer because he left no letters, diaries, or other private writings containing his personal views; instead, he left plays, and in a good play the actors do not speak for the dramatist but for the characters they are impersonating. The audience cannot, then, say that Shakespeare approved of evil because he created murderers or advocated religion because he created clergymen; we cannot say that he believed in fatalism because he created fatalists or admired flattery because he created flatterers. All these would be naive, and contradictory, reactions to the plays. Shakespeare's characters represent such a vast range of human behavior and attitudes that they must be products of his careful observation and fertile imagination rather than extensions of himself. A critic named Desmond McCarthy once said that trying to identify Shakespeare the man in his plays is like looking at a very dim portrait under glass: The more you peer at it, the more you see only yourself.

One thing is certain: Shakespeare was a complete man of the theater who created works specifically for his own acting company and his own stage. He had, for instance, to provide good parts in every play for the principal performers in the company, including the comedians acting in tragedies. Because there were no actresses, he had to limit the number of female parts in his plays and create them in such a way that they could readily be taken by boys. For instance, although there are many fathers in the plays, there are very few mothers. Although boys could be taught to flirt and play shy, acting maternally would be difficult for them. Several of Shakespeare's young women disguise themselves as young men early in Act I—an easy solution to the problem of boys playing girls' parts. Shakespeare also had to provide the words for songs because theatergoers expected singing in every play; furthermore, the songs had to be devised so that they would exhibit the talents of particular actors with good voices. Because many of the plays contain many characters, and because there were a limited number of actors in the company, Shakespeare had to arrange for doubling and even tripling of roles; that is, a single actor would have to perform more than one part. Because, of course, an actor could impersonate only one character at a time, Shakespeare had to plan his scenes carefully, so that nobody would ever have to be onstage in two different roles at the same time. A careful study of the plays shows that Shakespeare handled all these technical problems of dramaturgy masterfully.

Although the plays are primarily performance scripts, from earliest times the public has wanted to read them as well as see them staged. In every generation, people have felt that the plays contain so much wisdom, so much knowledge of human nature, and so much remarkable poetry that they need to be pondered in private as well as enjoyed in public. Most readers have agreed with what the poet John Dryden said about Shakespeare's "soul": The man who wrote the plays may be elusive, but he was obviously a great genius whose lofty imagination is matched by his sympathy for all kinds of human behavior. Reading the plays, then, is a rewarding experience in itself; it is also an excellent preparation for seeing them performed on stage or on film.

Shakespeare's contemporaries were so eager to read his plays that enterprising publishers did everything possible, including stealing them, to make them available. Of course the company generally tried to keep the plays unpublished because they did not want them performed by rival companies. Even so,

eighteen plays were published in small books, called *quartos,* before Shakespeare's partners collected them and published them after his death. This collection, known as the *first folio* because of its large size, was published in 1623. Surviving copies of this folio are regarded as valuable treasures today. But of course, the general reader need not consult any of the original texts of Shakespeare because his works never go out of print; they are always available in many different languages and many different formats. The plays that exist in two different versions (one in a quarto and one in the folio) have provided scholars with endless matter for speculation about what Shakespeare actually intended the correct text to be. Indeed, every aspect of Shakespeare has been, and continues to be, thoroughly studied and written about by literary and historical scholars, by theater and film people, by experts in many fields, and by amateurs of every stripe. No wonder he is mistakenly regarded as a great mystery.

The Renaissance Theater

By the mid-sixteenth century, the art of drama in England was three centuries old, but the idea of housing it in a permanent building was new, and even after theaters had been built, plays were still regularly performed in improvised spaces when acting companies were touring the provinces or presenting their plays in the large houses of royalty and nobility.

In 1576, James Burbage, the father of Shakespeare's partner and fellow actor Richard Burbage, built the first public theater and called it, appropriately, the Theater. Shortly thereafter, a second playhouse, called the Curtain, was erected. Both of these were located in a northern suburb of London, where they would not affront the more staid and sober-minded residents of London proper. Then came the Rose, the Swan, the Fortune, the Globe, the Red Bull, and the Hope: an astonishing number of public theaters and far more than there were in any other capital city of Europe at that time.

The Globe

The Globe, of course, is the most famous of these because it was owned by the company to which Shakespeare belonged. It was built out of timbers salvaged from the Theater when the latter was demolished in 1599. These timbers were carted across London, rafted over the Thames, and reassembled on the Bankside near a bear garden where bears were baited—not the most elegant of London suburbs. Since many of Shakespeare's plays received their first performances in the Globe, curiosity and speculation about this famous building have been common for the last three hundred years or more. Unfortunately, the plans for the Globe have not survived, though there still exist old panoramic drawings of London in which its exterior is pictured, and there is still considerable information available about some other theaters, including a sketch of the Swan's stage and the building contract for the Fortune. But the most important source of information are the plays themselves, with their stage directions and other clues to the structure of the theater.

The Structure of the Globe

At the present time, most scholars accept as accurate the reconstruction of the Globe published by C. Walter Hodges, whose drawing appears on page 284 in The Renaissance Theater section of *Elements of Literature: Sixth Course*. The theater in this drawing has three main parts: the building proper, the stage, and the tiring house (or backstage area), with the flag flying from its peak to indicate that there would be a performance that day.

The theater building proper was a wooden structure three stories high surrounding a spacious inner yard open to the sky. It was probably a sixteen-sided polygon. Any structure with that many sides would appear circular, so it is not surprising that Shakespeare referred to the Globe as "this wooden O" in his play *Henry V*. There were probably only two entrances to the building, one for the public and one

for the theater company, but there may well have been another public door used as an exit because when the Globe burned down in 1613, the crowd all escaped the flames quickly and safely. General admission to the theater cost one penny; this entitled a spectator to be a groundling, which meant that he or she could stand in the yard. Patrons paid a little more to mount up into the galleries, where there were seats and where there was a better view of the stage, along its two sides; people who wanted to be conspicuous rented them, and they must have been a great nuisance to the rest of the audience and the actors. A public theater could hold a surprisingly large number of spectators: three thousand, according to two different contemporary accounts. The spectators must have been squeezed together, and so it is no wonder that the authorities always closed the theaters during epidemics of plague. The stage jutted halfway out into the yard so that the actors were in much closer contact with the audience than they are in modern theaters, most of which have picture-frame stages with orchestra pit, proscenium arch, and front curtains. A picture-frame stage usually attempts to give the illusion of reality: Its painted scenery represents the walls of a room or an outdoor vista, and the actors pretend that nobody is watching them perform, at least until it is time to take a bow. To be sure, theater designs have been changing since World War II, and people have again learned to enjoy plays "in the round," without elaborate realistic settings. Modern audiences are learning to accept what Renaissance audiences took for granted: that the theater cannot show reality. Whatever happens on the stage is make-believe. Spectators at the Globe loved to see witches and devils emerge through the trapdoor in the stage, which everybody pretended led down to hell, though everybody knew that it did not, just as everybody knew that the ceiling over part of the stage was not really the heavens. This ceiling was painted with elaborate suns, moons, and stars, and it contained a trapdoor through which angels, gods, and spirits could be lowered on a wire and even flown over the other actors' heads. Such large sensational effects as these were plentiful in the Renaissance theater. At the opposite extreme, every tiny nuance of an individual actor's performance could affect the audience, which was also very close to the stage. The actors were highly trained, and they could sing, dance, declaim, wrestle, fence, clown, roar, weep, and whisper. Unfortunately, none of this liveliness can be conveyed by the printed page; we must imagine all the activity onstage as we read.

The third structural element in this theater was the tiring house, a tall building that contained machinery and dressing rooms that provided a two-story back wall for the stage. Hodge's drawing shows that this wall contained a gallery above and a curtained space below. The gallery had multiple purposes, depending on what play was being performed. Spectators could sit there, musicians could perform there, or parts of the play could be acted there. Many plays have stage directions indicating that some actors should appear on a level above the other actors—on balconies, towers, city walls, parapets, fortifications, hills, and the like. The curtained area below the gallery was used mainly for "discoveries" of things prepared in advance and temporarily kept hidden from the audience until the proper times for showing them. In Shakespeare's *The Merchant of Venice*, for example, the curtain is drawn to reveal (or "discover") three small chests, in one of which is hidden the heroine's picture. Some modern accounts of Renaissance theaters refer to this curtained area as an inner stage, but apparently it was too small, too shallow, and too far out of the sight of some spectators to be used as a performance space. If a performer were "discovered" behind the curtains, as Marlowe's Dr. Faustus is discovered in his study with his books, he would quickly move out onto the stage to be better seen and heard. Thrones, banquets, beds, writing desks, and so on could be pushed through the curtains onto the stage, and as soon as a large property of this sort

appeared, the audience would know at once that the action was taking place indoors. When the action shifted to the outdoors, the property could be pulled back behind the curtain.

Scenery

The people in the audience were quite prepared to use their imaginations. When they saw actors carrying lanterns, they knew it was night, even though the sun was shining brightly overhead. Often, instead of seeing a scene, they heard it described, as when a character exclaims,

> But look, the morn in russet mantle clad
> Walks o'er the dew of yon high eastward hill.
> —*Hamlet*
> Act I, Scene 1

Shakespeare could not show a sunrise; instead of trying to, he wrote a speech inviting the audience to imagine one. When the stage had to become a forest, as in several of Shakespeare's comedies, there was no painted scenery trying (and usually failing) to look like real trees, bushes, flowers, and so on. Instead, a few bushes and small trees might be pushed onto the stage, and then the actors created the rest of the scenery by speaking poetry that evoked images in the spectators' minds. In *As You Like It*, Rosalind simply looks around her and announces, "Well, this is the Forest of Arden."

The great advantage of this theater was its speed and flexibility. The stage could be anywhere, and the play did not have to be interrupted while the sets were shifted. By listening to what was being said, the audience learned all that they needed to know about where the action was taking place at any given moment; they did not need to consult a printed program.

Act and Scene Divisions

Most of the act and scene divisions in Renaissance drama have been added by later editors, who have tried to adapt plays written for the old platform stage to the modern picture-frame stage. In this process, editors have badly damaged one play in particular, Shakespeare's *Antony and Cleopatra*. This play was published and republished for a hundred years after Shakespeare's death without any act and scene division at all. Then one editor cut it up into twenty-seven different scenes and another into forty-four, thus better suiting the play to the picture-frame stage, or so they thought. But a stage manager would go mad trying to provide realistic scenery for this many different locales. Even a reader becomes confused and irritated trying to imagine all the different places where the characters are going according to the modern stage directions, which are of a kind that Shakespeare and his contemporaries never heard of. "Theirs was a drama of persons, not a drama of places," according to Gerald Bentley, one of our best theatrical historians.

Props and Effects

Some modern accounts have overemphasized the bareness of Renaissance theaters; actually, they were ornate rather than bare. Their interiors were painted brightly, there were many decorations, and the space at the rear of the stage could be covered with colorful tapestries or hangings. Costumes were rich, elaborate, and expensive. The manager-producer Philip Henslowe, whose account books preserve much important information about the early theater, once paid twenty pounds, then an enormous sum, for a single cloak for one of his actors to wear in a play. Henslowe's lists of theatrical properties mention, among other things, chariots, fountains, dragons, beds, tents, thrones, booths, wayside crosses. The audience enjoyed the processions—religious, royal, military—that occur in many plays. These would enter the stage from one door, pass over the stage, and then exit by the other door. A few quick costume changes in the tiring house, as the actors passed through, could double and triple the number of people in a procession. Pageantry, sound effects, music both vocal and instrumental—all these elements helped give the audience their money's worth of theatrical experience.

Private Halls and Indoor Theaters

These, then, were the chief features of the public theaters that Renaissance dramatists had to keep in mind as they wrote their plays. In addition to these theaters, the acting companies also performed in two other kinds of spaces: in the great halls of castles and manor houses, and in certain indoor theaters in London (which are called indoor theaters to distinguish them from theaters like the Globe, which were only partly roofed over).

For performances in a great hall, a theater company must have had a portable booth stage. Temporary stages could easily accommodate any play written for the public theater except for scenes requiring the use of heavens overhanging the stage.

Something like this booth stage may also have been used in the private theaters like the Blackfriars, which Shakespeare's company, the King's Men, acquired in 1608. Although nothing is known about the physical features of the Blackfriars stage, we know that the building itself—a disused monastery—was entirely roofed over, unlike the Globe, where only part of the stage and part of the audience had the protection of a roof. One great advantage of Blackfriars was that the company could perform there in cold weather and, because artificial lighting always had to be used, at night. And so the King's Men could put on plays all during the year, with increased profits for the shareholders, among them Shakespeare.

About the Play

The Tragedy of Hamlet

Special Considerations

Possible sensitive issues in this play are mental instability, murder, judgements based on class, and self-destructive behavior.

For Viewing

Hamlet. Columbia/Tristar Studios, 1996, rated PG-13. This production was directed by Kenneth Branagh, with Kenneth Branagh and Kate Winslet starring as Hamlet and Ophelia.

Biography: William Shakespeare, Life of Drama. A & E Entertainment, 1996, not rated. A portrait of Shakespeare's life using documentation, historical accounts, and interpretations of his work.

Hamlet. Warner Studios, 1990, rated PG. This production stars Mel Gibson and Helena Bonham Carter and was directed by Franco Zeffirelli.

For Listening

Hamlet. Naxos Audiobooks, 1997. Audio CD. A presentation of music and scenes from Hamlet.

Hamlet. Modern Library, 1996. In association with the BBC, selections from *Othello, Hamlet, King Lear,* and *Macbeth* are presented. Two cassettes.

Hamlet. Bantam Doubleday Dell, 1993. In a dramatization for BBC Broadcasting, Kenneth Branagh plays Hamlet and co-directs an ensemble performance of the complete version of the play. Four cassettes.

Historical Context

The story of the murdered king is one that held particular appeal for the audiences of Elizabethan England, and it is a story that Shakespeare returned to again and again in his plays (for example, in *Julius Caesar* and *Macbeth,* whereas in *Hamlet,* the stage is set by the murder of the good king). The story's appeal might be best attributed to the political unrest in England during this and recent periods.

Elizabeth I, queen of England from 1558 to 1603, was the daughter of Henry VIII and Anne Boleyn. Elizabeth had been declared illegitimate after her mother was executed by Henry. Following Henry's death, his son Edward VI, a nine-year-old, became king. (Political power lay in the hands of certain members of the court's council of ministers.) During Edward's reign, the country moved slowly away from the Catholic absolutism that marked Henry's reign toward a more moderate Protestantism. A political struggle erupted, ending with Mary I, sister to Edward and Elizabeth and a devout Catholic, assuming the throne. Mary's rule was marked by years of violent persecution of Protestants. Over time, Mary's health began to fail, and because she had not given birth to an heir, Parliament reestablished Elizabeth in the line of succession in 1544. On Mary's death, Elizabeth became queen.

Although she showed outward conformity to Catholicism, Elizabeth had a strong moral commitment to Protestantism. She reestablished Anglicanism as the state religion, and her actions against the Catholic power structure escalated harshly, causing serious unrest.

Religious unrest was countered by general prosperity under Elizabeth's rule. She was a gifted and able leader, stabilizing labor conditions, reforming currency, encouraging manufacturing and commerce, establishing a strong navy, and putting in place a policy of peace.

Elizabeth never married, although she had several favorites in her court. By maintaining her status as a single monarch, she cleverly used the prospect of marriage to her as a tool for securing alliances with powers such as France and Spain. Toward the end of her reign, Elizabeth was emotionally stricken by the treason of her then favorite, Robert Devereaux, second Earl of Essex, a melancholy and brooding character who many see as the model for Hamlet.

14 | *The Tragedy of Hamlet*

Copyright © by Holt, Rinehart and Winston. All rights reserved.

Sources of the Play

Shakespeare's story of *Hamlet,* in its basic outline, had a number of antecedents. As we know it, the play seems to represent the happy result of Shakespeare's habit of taking existing plot materials with theatrical potential and shaping them quickly and efficiently for his own dramatic and commercial purposes. In Shakespeare's mature work, his choice of basic material seems to have been based on his desire to explore certain emotional and intellectual questions, while still satisfying the expectations of his regular audience for a good show. Shakespeare's originality, like that of Sophocles, lies in the way he found and adapted already existing stories and plots, infusing them with flesh and blood and spirit.

The origin of the Hamlet story lies in the dim past of Scandinavian legend. A Danish historian, Saxo Grammaticus, is credited with the earliest narrative account of a prince named Amlethus in his *Historia Danica.* Written at the beginning of the thirteenth century, this work draws on the stuff of legend and the Scandinavian sagas. Grammaticus's work, in turn, was adapted around 1576 by François de Belleforest in his *Histoires tragiques,* and it is this version that may have come to Shakespeare's attention. In it are such potential crowd-pleasing elements as murder, revenge, and madness, along with early variations of such characters as Claudius, Gertrude, Ophelia, Polonius, and Hamlet himself. There are some basic differences in plot detail: for one, the murder of the Old Hamlet character is public knowledge (his brother claims he did the dread deed when apprehending the old Hamlet as the king was about to murder the queen); second, young Hamlet, feigning madness for self-protection, is regarded as suspect by his uncle, who resolves to kill the prince once he can prove him sane.

Closer in time to Shakespeare is another source, a lost play, mentioned by several of Shakespeare's contemporaries and often attributed to the playwright Thomas Kyd, whose *Spanish Tragedy* (c. 1585–1587) also contains some possible source materials for *Hamlet.* Shakespeare's *Hamlet* was probably first performed around 1600.

What attracted Shakespeare to this ancient Danish tale of revenge? The answer is that Hamlet and the problems he faces in Denmark are, after all, not much different from the potential problems faced by any Renaissance ruler in Shakespeare's day. On the one hand, Hamlet sees the need for social stability and for orderly succession. He knows the importance of tradition, of loyalty to the kingdom. But Hamlet is conflicted by other sensitivities: He also knows he must be true to his individual intelligence. He knows that though stability in society is important, stability might very well hide "something rotten." This rottenness in Denmark is used by Shakespeare as a metaphor for the rottenness that can kill the human spirit. But this is not a play that calls for rebellion and the assertion of the individual conscience over society's demands. Remember that Shakespeare was above all an Elizabethan; nothing was more important to the Elizabethan than social order. The conflict in this play is much subtler—what to do when an orderly state is known to be rotten inside, when the only recourse seems to be murder, an act that a civilized prince finds personally abhorrent. It is a conflict, of course, that has become increasingly relevant in our own century.

Critical Responses

"The purpose of playing," says Hamlet, "was and is to hold, as 'twere, the mirror up to nature; to show virtue her own feature, scorn her own image, and the very age and body of the time his form and pressure" (Act III, Scene 2). In composing the text of *Hamlet,* Shakespeare managed to fashion a mirror that has reflected for subsequent generations images of their own particular experience and nature. Readings, interpretations, and critical responses to the play have varied widely from one age to the next, from one place to another. *Hamlet* seems able to reflect the form and shape, the light and shadow, of many particular times.

So, in an age of reason, we might see the play as demonstrating the plight of the rational man in an irrational society, or we might read myopic, if logical, criticism of *Hamlet* as a wild and unruly play with all kinds of loose ends.

In a romantic age, we might see the prince as the exotic, intuitive, moody hero, inclined to throw himself into experience, yet thwarted at every turn by hypocrites and fools.

The Victorians called for a virtually photographic approach to the problems of Hamlet; they placed a naturalistic emphasis on the problems and destiny of the prince.

In our time, when revolutions in manners, fashions, education, science, and politics are commonplace, the mirrors provided by *Hamlet* are many. Some of these mirrors are distorting; some are magnifying. Today, Hamlet himself often becomes the figure of doomed youth, growing up in a world he never made, overwhelmed by politics before he has a chance to breathe. In *Shakespeare Our Contemporary,* the Polish critic Jan Kott describes an extremely effective production of the play in Kraków, several weeks after a meeting of a Congress of the Soviet Communist Party. In this version of *Hamlet,* political crime was at the heart of the action, politics itself was the real mad-

ness, the state was a prison, and characters spent their time spying on each other.

From another angle of vision, *Hamlet* becomes a case study of neurosis, of mind in conflict with itself. Hamlet has also been interpreted as dramatizing the ups and downs of a manic-depressive. The psychiatrist and biographer of Freud, Dr. Ernest Jones, in another provocative and influential analysis of the play, sees *Hamlet* as a complex account "of a boy's love for his mother, and consequent jealousy of and hatred toward his father." In his film of *Hamlet,* Sir Laurence Olivier offers similar Freudian interpretations.

James Joyce, in his great novel *Ulysses,* views Hamlet from another vantage point: Joyce has one of his main characters construct an interpretation of the play based on Hamlet's sense of profound loss at the death of his father.

In a version of the play performed at the Public Theater's New York Shakespeare Festival in New York in the late 1960s, Hamlet, in a discarded World War II bomber jacket, speaks "To be or not to be . . ." with a Puerto Rican accent. Ophelia, wearing a skimpy costume, in high heels and black stockings, belts out some of her lines into a hand-held mike like rock lyrics. The result is, as you might expect, an alienated, noisy, the-time-is-out-of-joint *Hamlet.*

Francis Fergusson, in his masterful study *The Idea of a Theater,* discusses a number of these reflections in Shakespeare's mirror. Fergusson's perspective on the play, encompassing a range of separate possibilities and interpretations, attempts to relate the richness of the play to the richness of our own times. At the center of the play, Fergusson focuses on the fact that "something is rotten in the state of Denmark," creating unrest and disorder and endangering the life of the body politic. Everything in *Hamlet,* some of it seemingly peripheral or irrelevant, Fergusson sees as related to the central conflict: the attempt to locate and destroy the source of the evil that is destroying society. Fergusson's analysis brings together the religious, philosophical, moral, political, and emotional aspects of the play in a scholarly and contemporary synthesis. Once again, we have a demonstration of the plenitude of Shakespeare's vision.

Much critical discussion focuses on the play as dramatic poetry, subordinating or even avoiding the reality of the play as a *dramatic* event, as a public *performance,* as a *play*. But if we lack an awareness of *Hamlet* as a performance, we will have only a blueprint, not a complete work of art. If we ignore the dramatic aspects of *Hamlet*, we are like people who imagine that, because they can read and understand a recipe, they will thereby know the look and flavor of that special celebration cake.

The following critical excerpts illustrate the range of critical discussion *Hamlet* inspires:

> Such mountains of commentary have been piled on *Hamlet* that we must remind ourselves to keep within the bounds of sanity: it is, after all, a play like any other play. Its Cambridge editor tells us that, the longest of all Shakespeare's plays, it is "the turning point of his spiritual and artistic development." If this seems a large claim we can agree that it is the beginning of those profound searchings of the soul, those explorations of territories on the ultimate limits of human experience, which are the great tragedies. These we can place beside only such comparable, if comparable, works as the Sistine ceiling of Michelangelo, the dynamic Panzer-divisions marching in Beethoven's mind.
>
> from *William Shakespeare: A Biography*
> A. L. Rowse

Hamlet is pound for pound, in my opinion, the greatest play ever written. It towers above everything else in dramatic literature. It gives us great climaxes, shadows, and shades, yet contains occasional moments of high comedy. Every time you read a line it can be a new discovery. You can play it and play it as many times as the

opportunity occurs and still not get to the bottom of its box of wonders. It can trick you round false corners and into cul-de-sacs, or take you by the seat of your pants and hurl you across the stars. It can give you moments of unknown joy, or cast you into the depths of despair. Once you have played it, it will devour you and obsess you for the rest of your life. It has me. I think each day about it. I'll never play him again, of course, but by God, I wish I could.

> from *On Acting*
> Sir Laurence Olivier

There would be no question at all in the minds of an Elizabethan audience that a murderer who could cheat his victims of their chance of salvation was a very bad man indeed; and indeed most of us would think with repulsion of such an action, if, through the hazards of war or dictatorship, it came within our experience.

But to this bad man Shakespeare ascribes one virtuous action; and the nature of that action is determined by his most lasting preoccupation. It is a political action. Hamlet gives his dying breath to thought for the future of his people; his last words choose a ruler for them. . . .

Hamlet was never more the Renaissance man—who was a statesman, a true Macchiavellian, a prince careful for the safety of his subjects. Even if one be disillusioned with the race, and suspect paragons and the beauty of the world, this is still admirable. These fragile creatures, so little changed from dust that they constantly revert to it, show bravery in their intention that their species shall survive as if it were marble. Yet, all the same, how horrid is the sphere in which they show their excellence. The court was saved by its political conscience; yet it was damned by it too.*

> from *The Court and the Castle*
> Rebecca West

From "The Nature of Will" ("The Court and the Castle") by Rebecca West. Copyright © by **Yale University Press.** Reprinted by permission of the publisher.

Hamlet is characterized chiefly by excess. The excess is an *embarras de richesses,* and criticism recently has tended to stress the embarrassment rather than the riches. The play has too much story and too many people; yet there is not enough story to explain all the people, and not enough people to tell the whole story. The effects gained are those of a brilliant opportunism. Shakespeare lends his pen to every occasion regardless. One result is that *Hamlet* contains more quotable phrases than any other of Shakespeare's plays, and more memorable scenes. Another result is a sense of bewilderment. In spite of all the things that are crowded in and which we would not be without, there is so much that seems to have been crowded out which we could certainly do with. The play has everything that Shakespeare can give, except the final synthesis: no one has been satisfied with Horatio's summary:

. . . give order that these bodies
High on a stage be placed to the view;
And let me speak to th' yet unknowing world,
How these things came about. So shall you hear
Of carnal, bloody, and unnatural acts;
Of accidental judgments, casual slaughters;
Of deaths put on by cunning, and forced cause,
And, in this upshot, purposes mistook
Fal, on the Inventor's heads: All this can I
Truly deliver.

> (*Hamlet,* Act V, Scene 2)
> from *Shakespeare's Doctrine of Nature*
> John F. Danby

Interpreting the Character of Hamlet

The range of approaches to *Hamlet,* from the elaborate to the lean, represents different attempts to deal with the basic problem in staging the play: finding the best means, under the circumstances presented by time, place, acting talent, and audience sensitivity, to create and convey a sense of life itself. At the heart of the solution is, of course, the style of the acting, and the focus there inevitably comes to rest on the way the key player deals with Hamlet himself.

Do we want a stylized, "classical" Hamlet, a "literary" creature out of the past? Or do we want a Hamlet natural in manner whose ups and downs make us feel at once the "shock of recognition?" Do we want to invite the audience to establish a sense of community with us? Or do we want possibly to alienate the audience by self-consciously presenting them with a "classic"—something that we, as the doctors in the case, imagine will be good for them? *Hamlet* has known—and survived—actors whose approach has been self-centered and operatic. To some stars, the soliloquies of Hamlet are so rich in their sound and imagery that they seem to invite star turns, actors who decide to play the scenes for all they themselves are worth, to extract all the juice from them, and to shower the audience with the glory of their own talent. Such virtuoso performers will draw applause and ovations, just as a tenor does after a celebrated Verdi aria. Such performers might also forget the play and leave their fellow actors to fend for themselves in a production that offers no consistency, no steady pulse, only occasional spasms of poetry. (Hamlet's own advice to the players shows us that Shakespeare was aware of the perils of overdoing things on stage.)

The following discussion of acting styles by Howard Taubman, a former drama critic for *The New York Times,* offers a lively survey of the acting approaches to *Hamlet,* culminating in an evaluation of Richard Burton's 1964 performance. The other excerpt here is by William Redfield, who played the role of Guildenstern in Burton's 1964 production and wrote a book on it during the considerable free time he had during rehearsals. Redfield gives us his own particular insights into the acting process.

*A Virile Hamlet:
No Sign of Neuroses in Burton's Prince
Howard Taubman

There probably are more ways to play Hamlet than are dreamt of in the philosophy of a theatergoer who thinks he has seen everything. Most of them no doubt have been tried on the world's stages in the last three and a half centuries, though someone somewhere will seek a new wrinkle.

Hamlets have sawed the air and split the ears of the groundlings, ignoring the very warnings that they speak to the players. There have been elegant, droopy, esthetic, posturing, tubercular, and Herculean Hamlets. Young matinee idols proud of a fine profile and a well-turned leg have orated the soliloquies as if they were speaking them into a looking glass, and venerable actors have declaimed the lines with a throbbing sonority that belied the instability of their rheumatic joints.

Richard Burbage, for whom Shakespeare wrote the part, must have been an uncommon actor, for the playwright, a practical man of the theater as well as a poet, designed a role shrewdly for a player's strength, and he surely knew that to play Hamlet a man must have physical suppleness and stamina, vocal range, alertness of intellect, a relish of the human comedy, awe of the mystery of life and death, and pity for the common tragic burden.

Garrick's Style

David Garrick, for all his tampering with Shakespearean texts, was intelligent enough to be welcomed in the company of Dr. Samuel Johnson, a man not given to suffering humbugs or numbskulls gladly. Garrick's style on the stage was direct and simple and helped to demolish the ranters and praters who had been in vogue.

Edmund Kean was a fiery actor, and his Hamlet was probably volatile and electrical, like a summer storm. Edwin Forrest belonged to the expansive, sonorous school, and Edwin Booth once again swung the pendulum in the other direction with the control and sensitivity of his playing.

Actors have run a gamut of Hamlets from the somberly introverted to the oracularly extroverted. There have even been female Hamlets. Sarah Bernhardt played the prince in her Paris theater at the turn of the century, as had Charlotte Cushman, one of our best actresses, in the middle of the nineteenth century. One supposes that the interpretations of these ladies were no more startling than some latter-day Hamlets who have drunk deeply of the troubled Freudian springs.

This Hamlet

Richard Burton's Hamlet is notable for his masculinity. Has there ever been a Hamlet so little sicklied o'er with the febrile cast of neurosis? He has a mind, and the turbulence of his thoughts is truly reflected in his "wild and whirling words."

But there is never a suggestion of madness. Claudius is uneasily aware that there is method in the seeming irrelevance of Hamlet's remarks, and even the foolish Polonius has faint intimations that a keen Hamlet is mocking him. Mr. Burton's Hamlet does not belie the descriptions Shakespeare put into the mouths of the other characters.

This Hamlet is full of the temperament of a man in prime physical and mental health. I, for one, am glad to meet such a Hamlet. He is, I think, Shakespeare's Hamlet. He makes understandable and credible all the good things said of him, like Ophelia's recollection of "a noble mind . . . the courtier's, soldier's, scholar's, eye, tongue, sword."

*From "A Virile Hamlet: No Sign of Neuroses in Burton's Prince" by Howard Taubman from *The New York Times,* April 19, 1964. Copyright © 1964 by the **New York Times Company.** Reprinted by permission of the publisher.

The Performance

The wit that lights up Hamlet's cold, penetrating eyes and leaps like quicksilver to his tongue is native to Mr. Burton's address and speech. The winning charm that once made him a good companion for his school fellows is entirely believable. And so is the quick perception of unworthy motives.

As an actor who can think, Mr. Burton appreciates the chances he takes in a Hamlet so tempestuous, yet fundamentally healthy. He knows that to let loose the full powers of his ringing voice is to risk being tumultuously rhetorical in a modern theater self-consciously addicted to whispers and mumbles. But the grand vocal style is not abused and does not become meretricious. Mr. Burton can scale it down to human size when he must be tender with Ophelia, anguished with his mother, and in painful communion with himself.

The admirable outcome of Mr. Burton's approach is that Hamlet's rashness, the flaw that undoes him, is the natural trait of a brilliantly gifted young man. The defect of this Hamlet is that there is insufficient contrast to justify hesitations after the play within the play has proved Claudius's guilt. When he stands over the praying king, sword poised, Hamlet refrains from striking without the subtle modulation of feeling that would make the movement humanly right rather than theatrical.

John Gielgud's staging supports and complements Mr. Burton's virile style. Actors of unusual experience fill most of the roles, and Hume Cronyn's Polonius is an unfaltering realization of aging garrulity and fatuity.

The decision to do the play in rehearsal clothes as if it were a final run-through on a bare, working stage may be useful to the directors and performers. If they feel that their energies and imaginations are liberated, one must grant them this freedom of approach.

But it is questionable whether it also liberates the audience's imagination. There is a clash between the appearance of the actors in working garb and the glorious, soaring language. There is a more clangorous dissonance in the utilitarian proscenium stage and the surging action. On an open, outthrust stage the discord could not be so harsh or disturbing.

Take it all in all, this Hamlet is not the caprice of a distinguished director and a highly publicized star. It is Shakespeare seen in a fresh, personal light and realized with manly sweep and power. It is an exciting, individual view of a masterpiece, whose secrets no one ever fully plumbs.

The New York Times
April 19, 1964

Plot

The plot of *Hamlet* centers on Hamlet himself—his problems, the complications that affect them, and the ways in which he seeks to resolve them. He has lost a father, seen his mother remarry shortly thereafter, and has no one with whom to share his despondency. Hamlet is then called on to avenge his father's murder at the hands of the father's brother—who is also Hamlet's uncle, his stepfather, and the new king of Denmark.

To put the main action in focus and to comment on it, Shakespeare uses subplots, the stories of Polonius and Laertes and of Fortinbras, father and son. These characters share Hamlet's main concerns—the father-son relationship and revenge.

There is also a wider frame in which Hamlet's drama is played. From this perspective, the plot focuses on the fact that the natural order of things, social harmony and truth in human relations, have been subverted and corrupted through "foul and most unnatural murder" and the takeover of the state, with the perpetrator unknown, undiscovered, hidden from the light of justice. "Something is rotten in the state of Denmark," and everyone is affected by it, breathing in a "pestilent congregation of vapors" as the health of normal affiliations deteriorates. Families disintegrate, friendships dissolve in betrayal, madness and suicide become familiar. The quest to discover the source and reveal it to the people, thus restoring the natural order, falls to Hamlet as a kind of avenging angel. His resulting actions define the development and dimensions of the tragic plot.

Accordingly, one can consider Hamlet's tragic flaw as procrastination, or his being "sicklied o'er with the pale cast of thought"—he thinks too much when he should be acting. Or perhaps his flaw is that he is called on to do the one thing he is not truly equipped for, as a civilized man. At the same time, we see the tragic condition in which all are affected, caught up in something much larger, all-pervasive, and deadening in its effects on good and evil, innocent and guilty alike. Perhaps the emphasis on a tragic fault or two oversimplifies the complexity of Hamlet's personality and the situation in which he finds himself. If only he didn't procrastinate so much, these things wouldn't have happened. If only he had made up his mind once and for all earlier, perhaps these deaths would have been avoided. But the tragic plot is somehow thicker than that and retains its own mystery.

A **Literary Elements Worksheet** that focuses on **plot** appears on page 110 of this Study Guide

A **Literary Elements Worksheet** that focuses on **conflict** appears on page 106 of this Study Guide

A **Reading Strategies Worksheet** that focuses on **summarizing** plot elements appears on page 73 of this Study Guide

A **Reading Strategies Worksheet** that focuses on **determining cause and effect** appears on page 89 of this Study Guide

A **Play Review Worksheet** that focuses on **character, setting, plot,** and **theme** appears on page 104 of this Study Guide

Setting

Hamlet is set in the Danish seaport of Elsinore, located on the narrow straits between Denmark and Sweden. Because of its location on an important trade route, Elsinore was well known to people of Elizabethan England. Kronborg, a fortress used for collecting tolls from ships entering or leaving the Baltic Sea, was likely the structure envisioned by Shakespeare as the royal castle of the king. The rooms of the castle and its surrounding walls provide the setting for every scene except Act V, Scene 1, which takes places in a nearby graveyard.

English acting companies are known to have traveled to Elsinore during 1585 and 1586, and some scholars suggest that Shakespeare may have been among those actors, providing him firsthand knowledge of the setting. Others argue that factual errors in descriptions of the setting (for example, there is no "cliff/That beetles o'er his base into the sea") indicate that he never visited the site.

Style—The Poetry of *Hamlet*

Shakespeare employs blank verse—ten-syllable lines, unrhymed, divided into five measures of two beats, the second of which gets the accent. Because the ten syllables, with the even beats stronger than the odd, create a basic pulse or underlying rhythm, we may respond emotionally to the dialogue in the way we respond to music. The words are set down with a feeling for emphasis, dynamics, and changes in emotional tempo, and the composition that results has its own unique quality with the power to move us whether we understand all the words or not.

A brief comparison of passages illustrates Shakespeare's mastery of the basic form and something of his musicianship. There is no mechanical assemblage of beats and accents, no slavish adherence to pattern. Rather, one finds a flexible series of dynamic changes reflecting each speaker's own attitude and aim. Compare such contrasting passages as Polonius giving instructions to Reynaldo on how he should spy on Laertes at college (Act II, Scene 1), Ophelia's description of "mad" Hamlet's visit to her, as she reports to her father (Act II, Scene 1), and Claudius, alone, meditating on his guilt (Act III, Scene 3).

Another element that goes into the poetry of *Hamlet* is the **imagery.** Shakespeare uses imagery to help us hear and see more clearly. The images he creates enable us to visualize the play's ideas and themes. The images define such matters for us with a special immediacy, making abstractions come alive by calling to mind familiar aspects and phenomena of our experience. For Hamlet the world has become a depressing place and he is miserable. To express that

A **Literary Elements Worksheet** that focuses on **imagery** appears on page 109 of this Study Guide

feeling, he speaks of an "unweeded garden" with "things rank and gross [possessing] it merely." Later, when Hamlet appears to have lost his reason, Ophelia bemoans the loss of "Th' expectancy and rose of the fair state." And subsequently, when Ophelia lapses into madness, her lines are filled with fragmented images of the flowers that are not to be in this Denmark.

Major Characters

Hamlet is the son of the dead King Hamlet of Denmark and nephew/stepson of the present king, Claudius. Hamlet has returned to Elsinore from his studies in Wittenberg because of his father's death.

Claudius, the brother of Hamlet's dead father, assumed the throne after marrying his brother's widow, Gertrude. Although as a leader he is strong and effective in managing Denmark's external affairs, Claudius is essentially corrupt and emerges as a dangerous antagonist.

Gertrude, Hamlet's mother, is the widow of Old Hamlet and the wife of her former brother-in-law, Claudius. Although on first reading Gertrude may seem to be a weak character, she is, in fact, complex, exhibiting not only corruption, but also clear-sightedness and considerable courage.

Polonius is the Lord Chamberlain of the court and Claudius's chief advisor. The father of Laertes and Ophelia, Polonius is portrayed as a meddlesome busybody, overconcerned with his own position and with what he considers the proper behavior of his children.

Laertes is the son of Polonius. He has returned to Denmark from France for Claudius's coronation and emerges as a slightly stuffy, overprotective brother to Ophelia. As the play progresses, Laertes unwittingly becomes the instrument of Claudius's treachery.

Ophelia is the daughter of Polonius and the sister of Laertes. Based on various references, she was courted by Hamlet before the action of the play begins. Hurt by Hamlet's cruel rejection and shocked by her father's untimely death, Ophelia is driven to madness.

Horatio is Hamlet's most loyal friend in the play. He is the first to reveal news of the Ghost to Hamlet, and he serves as Hamlet's confidant in the showdown with Claudius. Some of the play's most memorable imagery is contained in Horatio's speeches.

Rosencrantz and **Guildenstern** are boyhood friends of Hamlet. Pliant and unctuous in their scenes with the king, they are easily exposed by Hamlet as hypocrites. These two characters lack distinctive individuality and are no match for Hamlet's insight and verbal ingenuity.

A **Reading Strategies Worksheet** that focuses on **making inferences** about characters appears on page 65 of this Study Guide

A **Reading Strategies Worksheet** that focuses on **organizing information** about characters appears on page 97 of this Study Guide

Fortinbras is the son of the late king of Norway (Old Fortinbras) and the nephew of the present king, a situation that presents a striking parallel with that of Hamlet. Originally portrayed as an impetuous adventurer, Fortinbras ironically becomes the leader of all Denmark at the end of the play.

The **Ghost** is the spirit of Old Hamlet, former king of Denmark and victim of his treacherous brother, Claudius. Although literally a sketchy character, Old Hamlet is recalled as a strong, courageous ruler and a paragon of manhood. The Ghost's demand for revenge sets in motion the events that result in a tragic end.

Themes

Appearance versus reality: Throughout the play, Shakespeare provides examples of things not being what they seem. Murderers appear to be innocent and solicitous; friends and lovers prove to be untrustworthy; the appearance of a ghost strains the boundaries of reality; and sanity masquerades as madness.

Life as theater: In this, as in other plays, Shakespeare draws on the metaphor of the world as a stage. Characters seem not to know who is true and who is acting, what is true and what simply passes for truth. The play-within-a-play in Act III emphasizes this theme.

Corruption, disease, and death: Discovering the source of evil is at the heart of *Hamlet* and touches virtually every action, from the Ghost walking about when he should be resting in peace, to the mental illness of Ophelia, and on to the poisons used by Claudius to corrupt the health of the state by destroying his brother the king and by attempting to do the same with Hamlet. The cure for the sickness of soul and state can be achieved only when the source of evil is brought to light, a task that falls to the avenging Hamlet.

Parents and children: *Hamlet* is about *family* relationships, especially those of fathers and sons—Hamlet father and son, Polonius and Laertes, and Fortinbras father and son—but also father and daughter—Polonius and Ophelia—and mother and son—Gertrude and Hamlet. The play raises questions about loyalty and duty and trust—somewhat comically when Laertes must listen to Polonius's counsel before returning to college and less comically when Ophelia is affected adversely by Polonius's injunctions regarding her behavior with Hamlet. With the character of Gertrude, the questions are compounded: Where, precisely, does the son's loyalty, duty, and trust lie now that his father has died, his mother has quickly remarried, and his stepfather has become man of the house and master of the kingdom?

A **Literary Elements Worksheet** that focuses on **theme** appears on page 107 of this Study Guide.

A **Literary Elements Worksheet** that focuses on **irony** appears on page 108 of this Study Guide.

The Play at a Glance *(cont.)*

The Tragedy of Hamlet

Revenge: In *Hamlet* Shakespeare offers psychological, spiritual, and political variations on the theme of revenge, as Hamlet, Laertes, and Fortinbras each seek to avenge his father's killing. The revenge tragedy was a popular dramatic genre in Renaissance England, with writers such as Kyd, Chapman, and Tourneur developing versions of what apparently was the more basic model, the plays of the ancient Roman tragedian Seneca.

The relationship of thought to action: Throughout the play, Hamlet struggles with balancing thought and action, and his fluctuations between apparent madness and sanity can be considered an offshoot of this relationship. Ophelia reinforces the theme with her descent into madness, providing a foil to Hamlet's "antic disposition" and, some would argue, feigned insanity.

Copyright © by Holt, Rinehart and Winston. All rights reserved.

Study Guide **25**

Introducing the Play

Options

RESEARCH

Who's Next in Line?

Divide the class into large groups, and assign each a modern-day monarchy to research and discuss. Examples are England, Jordan, Monaco, Japan, Denmark, and Sweden. Ask students to focus their research and discussion on the lines of succession. Encourage group members to speculate about why rules of succession were developed. Finally, have each group present its findings to the class. Invite a class discussion of the benefits and drawbacks of each method of succession. Point out that the question of who assumes the throne after a ruler's death is an issue in *Hamlet*.

AUDIOVISUAL INTRODUCTION

Just a Pique

Pique your students' interest by showing them a short clip from the beginning of one of the recent motion picture productions of *Hamlet*. Then, encourage a class discussion of what appears to be happening and how the story is likely to unfold. List these responses and predictions, and keep them on display as a basis for discussion during the reading of *Hamlet*.

JOURNAL ENTRY

It's Just Not Like That!

Have students think of a time when they were mistaken or fooled by appearances—when a person, a place, or an event turned out to be other than it seemed at first. Ask them to write journal entries describing the events leading up to their discovery, and elaborating on how the experience made them feel. Encourage students to conclude with what they learned from the experience. These responses do not need to be shared with the class or teacher.

RESEARCH

Where in the World?

Share with students that *Hamlet* is set in Elsinore, Denmark. References throughout the play are made to travel between Elsinore and Wittenberg, Germany; France; and England. Invite students to locate these cities and countries on a map and determine possible travel routes to Elsinore. Challenge groups of students to research what was happening in each country during the sixteenth and early seventeenth centuries to determine possible underlying themes. For example, the university at Wittenberg, where Hamlet studied, was the seat of Martin Luther's Protestant Reformation in the sixteenth century. A short time later, England's Protestant Queen Elizabeth I struggled in her attempt to reduce the influence of the Catholic Church.

LANGUAGE

Famous Lines

Hamlet is especially rich in phrases that have become a part of our everyday language. These lines often seem to clarify a point or conclude an issue with such a special sense of rightness that we use them without being aware of their origin. Such phrases demonstrate how a great poet can create the very stuff that helps us define our lives. Invite students to paraphrase or write briefly about the phrases below. Students might keep a diary of phrases that they feel are important or pertinent to their lives as they read the play.

"In my mind's eye . . . " (Hamlet; I, 2)

"This above all—to thine own self be true . . . " (Polonius; I, 3)

"To the manner born . . . " (Hamlet; I, 4)

"The cat will mew, and dog will have his day." (Hamlet; V, 1)

Some teachers like to plunge their students immediately into a brief "performance" of the play. If you want to try this, assign parts for an informal performance of the opening scene of Act I—the encounter with the Ghost during the cold night watch on the ramparts of Elsinore Castle.

Don't have a rehearsal; just get five students up in front of the class, books in hand, and have them read their parts. You can have several groups take turns performing the scene. However you handle this first "performance" of the play, the purpose is the same: to make students realize that they are studying a play meant to be *performed* in front of an audience. You'll undoubtedly be surprised at how quickly the students will catch on to the mood of the scene. With a few of these impromptu performances, some of the hurdles to the language will be cleared.

When you assign the reading of Act I, go over the format of the text carefully. Show students that unfamiliar words, phrases, and allusions are marked with a symbol and explained in a footnote that is keyed to the appropriate line number. Next, read a few of the Guided Reading questions, which begin on page 48 of this guide. Explain that these questions aid understanding by pointing to details of the plot and eliciting interpretations of character, language, and staging.

Use the first class period after students have read the act to allow them to *hear* Shakespeare's language. Read the opening scene yourself, play a sound recording, or show a film. Doing so will provide a model of correct phrasing and will show how much an actor's interpretation adds to the play's meaning.

A resource that is full of good ideas about teaching the play by means of performance is the Folger Library's *Shakespeare Set Free,* edited by Peggy O'Brien (Washington Square Press, published by Pocket Books.)

Understanding the Literary Elements

Remind students of the genre they are studying: Drama is a literary *and* a performing art. *Hamlet,* though written to be acted, is splendid reading. As you read, play recordings, and show films, students should see how gestures, timing, staging, sound effects, and actors' interpretations can affect meaning. Although the words do not change from performance to performance, the audience's perceptions and reactions do. The questions and exercises in the Study Guide will help students appreciate Shakespeare's mastery of dramatic structure and literary techniques. By reading and studying this play, students should come to see how Shakespeare keeps the audience's interest—how he alternates scenes of psychological subtlety with emotional peaks, how exquisitely he uses language, filling his verse with irony, imagery, and vivid figures of speech.

Establishing a Procedure

Before you begin to teach the play, examine the teaching resources in this Study Guide; they provide a wealth of ideas for classroom work, homework assignments, projects, reports, and tests. If possible, obtain a film of *Hamlet,* as well as books and audio-visual materials about Shakespeare, his times, and the Globe Theater. Then, determine which projects and writing exercises you will assign at the beginning of the unit, decide how you will present each act, and prepare a daily reading and assignment schedule. If possible, allow at least four weeks for the study of the play.

Use the first two or three days to prepare students for the reading. Discuss the Focusing on Background (pages 6–13*)*, and enhance the historical information with filmstrips, films, or illustrated books. Do not let your students be intimidated by the poetry of the play; introduce terms and read passages aloud, but postpone scrutiny of the dramatic technique until they are interested in the play and more comfortable with

Reading and Performing Options *(cont.)* **The Tragedy of Hamlet**

its language. In the same way, briefly introduce the five-part structure of Shakespearean drama. In doing this, you will be providing students with a vocabulary for discussing form, which they will do with much more understanding as they follow the plot.

You may want to duplicate for students the following diagram and definitions:

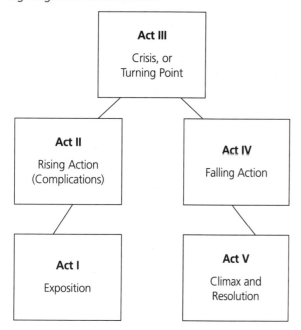

The **exposition** establishes the setting, introduces some of the main characters, explains background, and introduces the characters' main conflict.

The **rising action** is a series of **complications.** These arise when the protagonist takes action to resolve his or her main conflict.

The **crisis,** or **turning point,** is the moment of choice for the protagonist, when the forces of conflict come together, after which the situation either improves or inexorably deteriorates. The turning point is the dramatic and tense moment when the forces of conflict come together.

The **falling action** presents the events resulting from the action taken at the turning point. In tragedy, falling action necessarily emphasizes the play's destructive forces, but it often includes an episode of possible salvation as well as comic scenes. These are the playwright's means of maintaining the suspense and relieving the audience's tension as the catastrophe approaches.

The **resolution,** or **denouement,** is the conclusion of the play, the unraveling of the plot, which in tragedy includes the **catastrophe** of the hero's and others' deaths. The **climax,** or **climactic moment** of the play, is part of the denouement.

Finally, distribute your schedule for studying the play, and explain long-range projects and writing exercises. For example, if you want the class to undertake small-group activities, you should assign students to groups at this point so that they can begin to work together.

Here is a suggested procedure for presenting each act of the play. Before students begin to read, establish the time and place of each scene (if you desire, summarize the plot or distribute a plot summary); assign vocabulary words, discussion questions, and any writing exercises; designate passages for oral reading; alert students to any scenes for which you will play a recording; and remind students of quizzes and scheduled project reports.

Schedule at least two days of class time for each act. Vary activities from act to act as much as possible. The suggested combination of oral readings, discussion, viewing of scenes, and project reports should keep students stimulated throughout the course of the play.

After students finish reading the play, show a filmed production straight through; students will know the play very well by then, and the viewing will synthesize their experience of its elements.

Strategies for Inclusion

Use these ideas to modify your instructions to suit the needs of individual students.

Act I

English Language Learners Use frequent check tests to be sure students are comprehending the text. Ask students to stop at intervals and answer these or similar questions:

1. Who is speaking?
2. What is the character talking about?
3. To whom is the character speaking?
4. Who else is onstage?

Less Proficient Readers When you assign the reading of Act I, go over the format of the text carefully. Show students that unfamiliar words, phrases, and allusions are marked with a symbol and explained in a footnote by line number. Read aloud a few of the Guided Reading questions, which begin on page 48 of this guide, and explain that these questions aid understanding by pointing to plot details and eliciting interpretations of character, language, theme, and staging.

Visual/Linguistic To help students use prior knowledge to interpret the play, ask them to share their first thoughts on several main-idea words from Act I. List on the chalkboard, one at a time, such key words as *love, hate, revenge, reality,* and *lies.* From students' suggestions, make a cluster diagram like the following one.

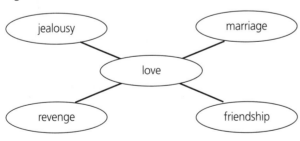

Spatial To help students track the sequence of events in the first scenes, ask them to write the five scene numbers at the tops of sheets of paper, one scene to a page (they may also want to use a different-colored sheet of paper for each scene). When they finish reading a scene, discuss the events as a class. Then, have each student write on his or her appropriately labeled sheet of paper a short summary of the action that has taken place. Students may also want to list on their scene pages the characters in the scene and add an illustration or a graphic organizer to help them keep the action of the story clear.

Auditory To provide a model of correct phrasing and to show students how much an actor's interpretation adds to meaning, read the opening scene aloud, play a recording, or show a film.

Act II

Spatial To help track the activity that takes place in Act II, have students make columns on a sheet of paper and then add the following headings: "A room in Polonius's house" and "A room in the castle." Then instruct them to take notes as they read, listing each event that occurs in each location.

Less Proficient Readers To focus students' attention on significant ideas and facts, provide a limited number of preview questions to be answered as the class reads Act II. Questions should be limited to sequential order. It may be helpful to have students copy down each question on a separate card and clip it to the page on which the answer can be found.

Kinesthetic Assign particular scenes to groups of two to four students, and ask the groups to perform their scenes as either skits or puppet shows. Puppets can be made by backing pictures from magazines with poster board and gluing the cutout figures to wooden sticks.

Auditory Explain to students that when they are reading a play, reading aloud or acting out the scenes is a helpful technique because often it will help them hear the tone of the dialogue. Read some scenes aloud; then, have students take turns reading selected scenes aloud. Assign reading parts ahead of time so students may practice before reading in class.

Advanced/Linguistic Ask interested students to review the soliloquy at the end of Act II and to write a soliloquy for Polonius or Ophelia. They may choose to write using Elizabethan language, or their soliloquies may be in modern English. Have students re-read Scene 1 to recall what would be appropriate for either character to say. Invite them to read their soliloquies aloud or post them in the classroom.

Act III

Less Proficient Readers Before students begin to read this act, review the style used in recording references to particular lines. Familiarity with the style will enable students to take notes more quickly and easily. Explain how lines are counted. Point out that in a split line, the number appears only once, even though the line includes the speech of two or more characters. Note that act numbers are represented by capital Roman numerals, and line and scene numbers by Arabic numerals. Remind students that the act number always appears first, the scene number second, and the line number third.

English Language Learners To help students follow the **plot,** have them keep a timeline of the events that take place. Pause periodically to review what has happened in the play.

Strategic Reading To encourage the class to examine events and speculate about their long-range consequences, have students stop at the end of Scene 1 and write a prediction journal entry. Tell students to draw a line down the middle of a sheet of paper. Have them write the heading *What Happened* on the left side, and the heading *What Might Happen As a Result of This Event* on the right side. Discuss students' predictions with the class. Then, after students read Scene 2, ask them to return to their journals and compare their predictions with what actually happened.

Speaking and Listening To develop students' metacognitive abilities, try an oral composition activity. Have each student choose a partner; then give each student in a pair a different interpretive essay question about the play (for example, How could an educated young man like Hamlet become consumed with the desire for revenge? Why do so many of the characters trust Horatio?). Tell students to take turns speaking (composing aloud an answer to a question) and listening (silently interpreting and recording the speaker's thoughts). Then, tell the students in each pair to exchange and discuss their notes.

Mechanics Explain to students that a dash is used to indicate a pause—an abrupt break in thought or speech, an unfinished statement or question, or an interruption by another character. Point out that pauses are used for dramatic effect. To demonstrate, ask students to read lines containing dashes as if the dashes were not there and then to read the same lines as written, with the dashes.

Interpersonal Remind students that Act III contains the play's turning point—the pivotal moment when the hero's fortunes begin to decline, setting in motion the play's falling action, which leads to its inevitable catastrophe. As they read, ask students to decide which event or decision constitutes this turning point. After the class has read the act, give pairs of students a self-adhesive note. Instruct each pair to mark the turning point by affixing the note next to the appropriate lines. Have students defend their choices to the class.

Special Needs Students having difficulty following the printed page might listen through headphones to an audiotape of the play. Encourage students who have difficulty participating in oral reading to develop other kinds of expertise during the study of the play. For example, they may become the class experts on authentic dress during the time of Hamlet by conducting research in the local or school library.

Visual To help students visualize the range of powerful emotions affecting characters in this act, ask them to collect and post illustrations to accompany several scenes. For example, students might gather magazine and newspaper photos that suggest hostility and anger among young men, anguish among grieving family members, fear and uncertainty in sweethearts, and impatience in parents and children. Have volunteers arrange illustrations brought to class on different-colored poster boards. Post the arrangements in the classroom.

English Language Learners Help students follow the action from scene to scene by periodically asking them to preface their speaking parts with a brief explanation of location. For example, before students begin to read a new dialogue, they can add a comment stating that the action is taking place in a room in the castle, a hall in the castle, or in the queen's room. Hearing the location of the action will help students shift from scene to scene.

Act IV

Advanced After students read Act IV, have them choose a character who could, at some point, have changed what has happened. Tell students to rewrite the scene at that point, showing how things would have happened had the character acted differently.

Visual/Auditory Have students work in small groups to create a computer-animated scene with sound. Each group should choose a short portion of a scene from the play. One student might be in charge of getting information on how the technology works, another might do the artwork, another might plan the animation, while another might create the sound.

Bodily-Kinesthetic Divide the class into two teams. Each team should prepare and then pose in five "frozen scenes." If the other team guesses the scene being represented on the first try, the presenting team gets five points. If the other team guesses it on the second try, the presenting team gets two; on the third try, one point. The team with the most points wins. Remind students to present material the audience sees.

Interpersonal In Act IV, new insights into the play's main characters are provided. Before beginning the act, have students work in pairs to create a character-

attribute cluster for Hamlet, Claudius, or Gertrude. Ask them to add new attributes to the cluster as they gain additional insights into their character in this act.

Auditory It is often expedient to arrive at reasons for or against a particular stance by articulating them in an informal debate. Have students work in pairs, and ask each partner to decide which side to take in the following debate: *Hamlet's determination to revenge his father's death is a force for good.* Turn on an audiocassette recorder, and tape the ensuing debate. Debaters should not initially be preoccupied with the logical soundness of their own arguments because this is a prewriting activity. A student should make a point, support it with evidence from the drama, and then allow his or her partner to rebut that point and counter with an opposing point. This process should continue until the debaters run out of points. The tape should be replayed, and the debaters may then record valid points for the debate.

Act V

Intrapersonal Ask students to imagine that Hamlet is their friend and to write a journal entry reacting to their friend's death.

Interpersonal Have students list words or phrases from the play that create connections with life today. Ask each student to share these connections with a partner. A volunteer recorder can make a composite list on craft paper titled "The Relevance of *Hamlet.*" To help students get started, suggest that they look for references concerning conflicts between generations, the rashness of youth, the hopelessness of forbidden love, or the destructive nature of revenge.

Special Needs Students with mobility limitations might enjoy working in the capacity of group technical adviser or director for a performance of the play. Remind groups that they will need one member to chart and oversee changes in the areas of lighting, volume, setting, and actor movement. A director who can observe rehearsals and make critical recommendations for improvements is essential. Students

Strategies
for Inclusion *(cont.)*

should be encouraged to pursue any role they find interesting.

English Language Learners Encourage students to participate in speaking lines even if they have doubts about their fluency in Shakespearean English. Those who wish to memorize parts and attempt the delivery of lines from a scene should be encouraged to practice with a self-selected partner. Remind students that all scene presentations will have strengths as well as some aspects that could be improved with additional experience.

Kinesthetic Many acting roles require the ability to stay motionless for some length of time. Some students may feel more comfortable and productive as active set designers or arrangers. Allow group members enough time to explore the demands of each task before committing themselves to making a specific contribution.

Intrapersonal As students consider the decision-making process that leads Hamlet to his death, have them complete an Options Tree. They should start with Hamlet's decision about whether to believe the Ghost's story and trace the path he follows through each decision he faces. Ask students to speculate in their Reader's Logs about how different things might have been if Hamlet had decided not to murder his uncle.

Bodily-Kinesthetic Allow interested students to demonstrate the dueling between Hamlet and Laertes. Students might demonstrate with cardboard or invisible foils.

Special Needs Ask students to consider why people still study *Hamlet* today. Guide them with the following questions: Did you learn anything from the downfall of Hamlet? Were there any **characters** you strongly liked or disliked, and why? What was Hamlet's flaw? Do any of the characters in the play remind you of people in today's society?

Plot Synopsis and Literary Elements

The Tragedy of Hamlet

Act I, Scene 1

Plot Synopsis

Sentries Francisco and Bernardo change shifts in their guard duty at midnight on a platform outside the royal castle in Elsinore. Horatio and Marcellus arrive to join Bernardo. The three men discuss the strange apparition that has twice appeared on the ramparts. Horatio doubts the others' report, but as Bernardo begins to describe it, the Ghost appears. Dressed in battle armor, the Ghost closely resembles Old Hamlet, the late king of Denmark. When Horatio demands that the Ghost speak, it stalks away.

Horatio suspects that the appearance of the Ghost in military dress signals some impending calamity for Denmark. The men discuss the strict watch and intensive military buildup of recent days. They speculate about rumors that young Fortinbras of Norway is mobilizing troops to reclaim the land his father, the late king of Norway, lost, along with his life, in a battle with Old Hamlet.

The Ghost reappears, and Horatio again implores it to speak, asking if there is some way they might help the Ghost rest in peace. The Ghost seems about to speak, but the cock crows, signaling daybreak, and the Ghost disappears. Horatio proposes that they tell young Hamlet, the dead king's son, what they have seen; perhaps the Ghost will speak to him.

Literary Elements

Mood: The opening scene is set at midnight in the dark, bitter cold of winter on the castle platform. By adding dialogue containing references to unexplained uneasiness, descriptions of war preparations in Denmark, and talk of a ghost, Shakespeare creates the ominous mood appropriate to a tragedy.

Motif: The brief exchanges among the guards on the castle platform suggest caution, distrust, and suspicion of treachery or disloyalty—motifs that will be present in the play as a whole. References to the Ghost introduce the motif of supernatural occurrences.

In medias res: Shakespeare uses the convention of *in medias res,* or beginning "in the middle of things." Horatio's speech explaining the contract between Old Fortinbras and Old Hamlet unobtrusively provides some important details of exposition in a flashback. Elements of the dialogue and the appearance of the Ghost also lead the reader to expect an explanation of events leading up to Old Hamlet's death.

Characterization: The characterization of Horatio, a scholar trained in Latin and knowledgeable in arcane matters, is notable for its language and imagery. Horatio has a number of famous lines in the play, including the personification near the end of the scene: "But look, the morn, in russet mantle clad/Walks o'er the dew of yon high eastward hill."

Although young Fortinbras is not directly introduced, his situation as a son determined to avenge his father's death furnishes a significant parallel to the predicament of Hamlet.

Theme: Horatio believes that the Ghost foreshadows "some strange eruption to our state," that is, some momentous calamity such as **death** and **destruction.** The Ghost appears to be that of Old Hamlet, but is it?

Act I, Scene 2

Plot Synopsis

King Claudius and Queen Gertrude enter a state room in the castle, along with Polonius, the Lord Chamberlain; Polonius's son Laertes; Hamlet, Gertrude's son and Claudius's nephew; and various members of the royal council. Claudius states that he has married Gertrude, the widow of his brother King Hamlet and his former sister-in-law, pointing out that he obtained approval of his court for this marriage (which otherwise would have been considered incestuous by canon law). Turning to state affairs, Claudius speaks of young Fortinbras, who demands the return of lands lost by his father to King Hamlet. Claudius reports that he is having Cornelius and Voltemand deliver a letter to Fortinbras's uncle, the bedridden king of Norway, asking the king's help in restraining young Fortinbras.

With official business completed, Claudius hears Laertes' request to return to France, where he lived prior to returning to Denmark for the coronation ceremonies. After determining that Polonius has given permission, Claudius agrees.

Claudius next addresses Hamlet, gently chastising him for still grieving over his father's death. When Hamlet bristles, Gertrude entreats her son to cease mourning, and Claudius points out that such excessive grief is impious and unmanly. Both Gertrude and Claudius urge Hamlet to remain in Elsinore rather than to return to school in Wittenberg, site of a famous German university. When Hamlet agrees, Claudius announces a celebration, and all but Hamlet exit.

In the soliloquy that follows, Hamlet reveals his private despair, noting that his distress stems not only from his father's death but also from his mother's hasty marriage to her brother-in-law. He condemns his mother and all women for moral weakness and inconstancy.

Horatio, Marcellus, and Bernardo enter. After commenting bitterly on his mother's remarriage, Hamlet begins to talk about his father, whereupon Horatio brings up the subject of the Ghost. Hamlet excitedly questions Horatio about the apparition and concludes that it might be his father's ghost or perhaps an evil spirit assuming his father's appearance. Swearing the three to secrecy, Hamlet declares that he will join the guards on their watch that night in an attempt to speak to the Ghost. After Horatio and the guards leave, Hamlet expresses his fear that the Ghost is a sign that "All is not well." He suspects that his father's ghost may have returned to earth to reveal a crime.

Literary Elements

Conflict: When Claudius refers to Hamlet as a cousin and a son and Hamlet responds "A little more than kin, and less than kind," [l. 65] he reveals the bitterness he feels toward his uncle. At this point, Hamlet recognizes the conflict as stemming primarily from Claudius's marriage to Gertrude. Hamlet deeply resents the marriage because of the implied disloyalty to Old Hamlet and because he sees the union as contrary to the laws of nature.

Antagonist: Early in the scene, Claudius emerges as Hamlet's antagonist—the character against whom Hamlet will struggle. He has not only replaced Hamlet's father as king (a role that might otherwise have fallen to young Hamlet) and hastily married his widow, but Claudius also seeks to retain the crown by subtly pointing out Hamlet's weaknesses and lack of ability to rule. Describing Hamlet so that all may hear with phrases such as "impious stubbornness," "a heart unfortified," and "a mind impatient," Claudius clearly is intent on strengthening his own position with the court.

Soliloquy: Hamlet has more soliloquies (long speeches in which a character who is usually alone onstage expresses his or her private thoughts) than any other tragic hero in Shakespeare. The first soliloquy occurs midway through this scene. We learn that Hamlet's grief at his father's death and his disgust at his mother's remarriage are so great that he wishes he could end his own life. He will continue with this train of thought with "To be, or not to be . . ." in a soliloquy in Act III, Scene 1.

Imagery: Hamlet's soliloquy in Act I is notable for its imagery relating to the theme of disease and corruption. These images of an unweeded garden overgrown with "things rank and gross" symbolize the corruption Hamlet perceives in the government and in the souls of those around him, particularly that of Claudius.

Theme: We see different relations between **parents** and **children** in this scene. Hamlet defers to his mother's request that he not return to the university, but in his soliloquy, he rails against her hasty remarriage. Clearly, he has conflicting feelings toward her. On the other hand, Laertes has badgered his father, Polonius, into permitting him to return to France.

Pun: Shakespeare liberally used the device of puns, that is, the play on multiple meanings of a word, in his plays. Hamlet's very first line, "A little more than kin, and less than kind," is an aside containing two puns. His phrase "more than kin" refers to his double relationship to Claudius, as a nephew and as a step-son; the word *kind* has the two meanings "kindly" and "natural." In his next two lines of dialogue, Hamlet makes puns on the words *sun* and *common*.

The association of Hamlet with puns throughout the play is significant for several reasons. On one level, his mastery of verbal play reveals his intellect and quick wit. On another, deeper level, his sensitivity to the nuances of language reflects his emotional sensitivity. Just as he can discern the multiple meanings of words, he is also the sort of man who considers many different sides of the same issue, a trait that will be revealed more fully in later soliloquies. Finally, Hamlet's fondness for puns is linked to his sensitivity to the ironic disparities between appearance and reality.

Act I, Scene 3

Plot Synopsis

In a room in Polonius's house, Laertes bids his sister Ophelia farewell. He advises her to be wary of Hamlet's recent attentions, telling Ophelia that Hamlet is not serious about her. He warns that, even if Hamlet's intentions were honorable, his position as prince places him far above her station socially and makes it impossible for him to choose a wife freely for himself. After being warned to protect her virtue, Ophelia playfully exhorts her brother to practice what he preaches.

Polonius enters and admonishes Laertes to hurry because the ship is waiting for him. After Laertes receives his father's advice and blessing, he departs. Then Polonius turns to Ophelia and interrogates her about her relationship with Hamlet. He ridicules as naive the notion that Hamlet is seriously interested in her, and he warns Ophelia not to make a fool of herself and of him. Polonius commands Ophelia to have no further contact with the prince, and she humbly agrees to obey her father's wishes.

Literary Elements

Characterization and Theme: Elements of the personalities of Polonius, Laertes, and Ophelia are indi-rectly revealed through the characters' speeches and actions in this scene. Laertes is portrayed as an affectionate, somewhat overprotective brother in his speech to Ophelia. His suspicions of Hamlet foreshadow possible future conflict. Ophelia, who is sometimes regarded as a flat or stereotyped character, shows by her retort to Laertes that she is capable of lightly ironic humor.

Polonius's speech to Laertes, full of clichés and banal moralizing, reveals Polonius as a pompous and rather foolish father; his speech to Ophelia shows that he has a suspicious, meddlesome nature and does not hesitate to bully his daughter. Completely ignoring Ophelia's assertions that there has been nothing dishonorable about Hamlet's behavior so far, he orders her to break off contact with Hamlet. Polonius seems oblivious to the likely effect of this demand on his daughter's feelings.

Foreshadowing: Shakespeare often provides clues to what may happen later in the plot. Polonius's insensitivity to his daughter's feelings in this scene foreshadows his willingness in Acts II and III to use Ophelia as a pawn in his plots to spy on Hamlet for the king.

Act I, Scene 4

Plot Synopsis

At midnight, Hamlet, Horatio, and Marcellus await the appearance of the Ghost on the guard platform outside the castle. When they hear the sound of trumpets and cannons, Hamlet explains that Claudius is holding a late-night celebration, with drinking, carousing, and dancing. He complains about the Danish custom of revelry, saying that it has given the Danes a contemptible reputation as swinish drunkards.

At this moment, the Ghost enters. Though unsure of whether it is truly his father's spirit or an evil demon, Hamlet begs the apparition to speak to him and explain why it has returned to earth. The Ghost beckons Hamlet to follow it, as if it has something to tell him in private. Marcellus and Horatio warn Hamlet not to follow, and they try to hold him back.

But Hamlet says he has nothing to fear. Threatening to "make a ghost" of anyone who hinders him, Hamlet exits with the Ghost. Fearing that Hamlet is in a desperate state, Horatio and Marcellus follow him.

Literary Elements

Mood: As in the first scene, the night setting on the guard platform creates suspense and an ominous mood of foreboding. The informal speeches in broken blank verse help to reinforce this mood.

Foreshadowing: Near the end of the scene, Marcellus's famous line, "Something is rotten in the state of Denmark," foreshadows the Ghost's revelations in the next scene. It also refers to the corruption of an entire people through the murder of the legitimate monarch and the usurpation of the throne.

Act I, Scene 5

Plot Synopsis

The Ghost addresses Hamlet, identifying itself as Hamlet's father's spirit, and bids Hamlet to listen attentively. The Ghost confides that King Hamlet died not from a serpent's sting as people thought but rather at the hand of the king's brother, Claudius, who poured poison in the king's ears while he slept in the orchard. Because Old Hamlet died without a chance to confess his sins or to receive the last rites, Claudius has doomed his victim's soul to walk the earth at night for a certain period of time and to suffer the torments of purgatory. The Ghost calls on Hamlet to avenge this horrible murder by killing Claudius, but he warns Hamlet not to taint his soul with the unnaturally cruel act of punishing his mother as well. As day breaks, the Ghost departs with the words, "Remember me," and Hamlet fervently vows to live only for revenge. With the help of the Ghost, he swears Horatio and Marcellus to secrecy.

Literary Elements

Conflict: The final scene of this act firmly establishes the principal conflict of the play: Hamlet is sworn to avenge his father's murder by killing Claudius, his uncle/stepfather, his mother's husband, and the ruling king of Denmark.

Theme: The meeting between Hamlet and the Ghost reinforces some of the play's principal themes. For example, the theme of **revenge** is explicit in Old Hamlet's dialogue with his son. As Hamlet's enthusiasm for revenge wakes to sober realization ("O cursed spite/That ever I was born to set it right"), it foreshadows the **relationship of thought to action** wherein Hamlet finds one reason after another to delay his **revenge.** A second major theme, that of things not being what they seem (**appearance versus reality**), is prominent toward the close, when Hamlet says that he may decide to feign madness by putting on an "antic disposition." The motif of corruption, so prominent in the imagery of the play, is raised to the level of a theme in Old Hamlet's lengthy description of Claudius's treachery and the physical effects of the poison.

Allusion: Much poetry from the period of the Renaissance contains allusions, or references, to both

Christian and pagan elements. Likewise, in this scene, the ghost of Christian King Hamlet, who has spoken of unconfessed sins and purgatory, refers to the mythological river Lethe. In Greek mythology, Lethe flowed through Hades and caused all who drank from its waters to forget their past.

Act II, Scene 1

Plot Synopsis

In a room at his house, Polonius instructs his servant Reynaldo on how to gather gossip about Laertes' conduct in Paris. First, he is to locate Danes who are living there, and then, through indirection and sub-terfuge, he is to bait them into acknowledging Laertes' wanton habits.

As Reynaldo sets off on his mission, Ophelia enters in a state of intense agitation. She tells Polonius that Hamlet came to her, wild and distraught, looking as if "he had been loosed out of hell/To speak of horrors." When Ophelia describes Hamlet's bizarre actions and appearance, Polonius is immediately convinced that Hamlet has gone mad because Ophelia has obeyed her father's bidding and spurned the young prince's atten-tions. Polonius decides that he should inform the king of Hamlet's dangerously desperate, lovesick condition.

Literary Elements

Characterization: Through his words and actions relating to Laertes, Polonius can be characterized as a suspicious, meddlesome busybody who is quick to think the worst of others—even his own son. These negative qualities are combined with limitations revealed in earlier scenes, including pomposity, cyni-cism, and insensitivity, and paint Polonius as a shallow and flawed individual.

Irony: For a man who prides himself on his cunning stratagems and superior insight, it is an instance of dramatic irony that Polonius is immediately taken in by Hamlet's pretense of lovesick madness.

Theme: The theme of **appearance versus reality** is reinforced by Hamlet's behavior in the brief meeting with Ophelia, which represents Hamlet's first effort to "act a part." Polonius instructs Reynaldo in the theme of **life as theater** as he tells him how to play the role of spy on Laertes.

Act II, Scene 2

Plot Synopsis

In a state room of the castle, Claudius and Gertrude welcome Rosencrantz and Guildenstern, boyhood friends of Hamlet's, and ask their help in learning what has caused such a change in Hamlet. The two young men agree and go off in search of Hamlet. Polonius enters, announcing the return of the ambas-sadors to Norway and confiding that he has discov-ered the cause of Hamlet's madness.

Attending first to state business, Claudius learns that the king of Norway has ordered Fortinbras to stop his military activity against Denmark but has requested permission for Fortinbras to pass through Denmark en route to a military action in Poland. After the ambassadors leave, Polonius declares that Hamlet has been driven mad by Ophelia's rejection of him. As part of his long-winded proof of this theory, he produces an eccentric love letter written by

Hamlet to Ophelia. When Claudius asks for further proof of this theory, Polonius suggests a scheme wherein he and Claudius will spy on an arranged meeting between Ophelia and Hamlet.

Hamlet enters and talks briefly with Polonius before contemptuously dismissing him. Hamlet then warmly greets Rosencrantz and Guildenstern and asks the reason for their return to Denmark. As the conversation continues, Hamlet grows increasingly suspicious of them and finally forces Rosencrantz and Guildenstern to confess that they are in Elsinore because the king and the queen have sent for them. Although Hamlet is disappointed in his old friends, he is interested in news they bring of an acting company that has just arrived in Elsinore.

The players enter, along with Polonius, and Hamlet requests that the First Player recite a lengthy speech from a play based on the *Aeneid*—a speech that recounts Hecuba's agony following the death of her husband King Priam. Then Hamlet privately asks the First Player to perform a play called *The Murder of Gonzago* the following night, including lines that Hamlet will write.

After all but Hamlet exit, he reveals that the lines he plans to write will contain details of a murder similar to that of his father. By Claudius's reaction to this part of the play, Hamlet will know whether the king is guilty of murdering Old Hamlet.

Literary Elements

Plot: The plans set in motion by Polonius and by Hamlet in this scene serve to advance the rising action. Suspense builds regarding Polonius's plan to spy on Hamlet and Hamlet's test of Claudius, an event that will mark the dramatic climax, or structural turning point, of the play.

Irony: Shakespeare ironically gives the long-winded and pompous Polonius a line that has become proverbial: "Brevity is the soul of wit." His rambling, however, earns a sharp reproof from Gertrude: "More matter, with less art." The audience will probably note a further irony in Hamlet's letter: It is written in clumsy, stilted verse, for which he apologizes. Its trite style is not at all what one would expect from the brilliant, articulate, and scholarly prince, and the letter's message is strange: Hamlet tells Ophelia not to doubt his love, but in Elizabethan English, *doubt* can also mean "suspect."

Allusion: The background for the Player's speech on Hecuba can be found in Book II of Virgil's *Aeneid,* where the epic hero Aeneas tells Dido, the Queen of Carthage, the story of the fall of Troy. Aeneas recounts how Pyrrhus, the son of the Greek hero Achilles, savagely killed old King Priam during the Greek sack of the city, while Queen Hecuba, Priam's wife, watched helplessly. Revenge perhaps played a part in the killing because Priam's son Paris had killed Achilles. Within the world of the play, Pyrrhus is like Claudius in that he is the ruthless murderer of a father; at the same time, he is like Hamlet, a son who feels bound to avenge the death of a father.

Soliloquy and Theme: Hamlet's soliloquy at the end of this scene reinforces the themes of **revenge** and of **appearance versus reality.** Hamlet stresses the difference between reality and a part played on the stage. Then, however, he goes on to express how playing and acting may, paradoxically, reveal the deepest truths about real life and human nature. He plans to use this ability of the theater to "catch the conscience of the King" through the performance of the play-within-a-play.

Act III, Scene 1

Plot Synopsis

Rosencrantz and Guildenstern report to Claudius that they have not learned the cause of Hamlet's madness. They add that Hamlet has expressed excitement about a group of traveling actors and has asked the troupe to perform a play at court. The king agrees to attend the performance.

A short time later, Polonius and Claudius prepare to spy on the "chance" meeting they have arranged between Hamlet and Ophelia. Hamlet enters and, before noticing Ophelia, delivers the famous "To be, or not to be" soliloquy. Catching sight of Ophelia, Hamlet assumes his pretense of madness. After denying feelings of love for Ophelia, he launches into a tirade against women's lust and duplicity. After Hamlet exits, Ophelia laments Hamlet's insanity and his bitter rejection of her. When Claudius and Polonius reenter, the king reveals that he is not entirely convinced that Hamlet is mad, and he suggests that Hamlet be sent to England. Polonius, eager to show that Hamlet's madness is caused by neglected love, asks to eavesdrop on a private conversation between Hamlet and his mother after the players' performance. Claudius agrees as the scene ends.

Literary Elements

Irony: In ironic parallel, Claudius and Hamlet prepare to test one another. Claudius reveals that he is not convinced that Hamlet's madness is genuine and plans to test his nephew by exploiting the prince's fondness for Ophelia, as well as his old friendship with Rosencrantz and Guildenstern. At the end of Act II, Hamlet put into place his plan to test the guilt or innocence of the king. Claudius's evident pleasure in hearing of Hamlet's interest in the players, who are part of Hamlet's test to "catch the conscience of the King," is an example of dramatic irony.

Characterization: The fact that Claudius, unlike Polonius and Gertrude, is suspicious of Hamlet's madness is consistent with his portrayal as an intelligent, formidable antagonist for the hero. Shakespeare paints Claudius as a complex personality and as a far more rounded character than the stereotypical Elizabethan stage villain.

Shakespeare portrays Hamlet in an unsympathetic, almost cruel light in this scene. Hamlet's rejection of Ophelia and his oblique mockery of womankind are perhaps psychological reflexes to the shock of his mother's remarriage, but Ophelia's hurt is palpable. Blaming Hamlet's behavior on his madness, Ophelia praises him as a courtier, soldier, and scholar.

Theme: Claudius uses imagery of violence and **corruption** to reveal his own sense of guilt in an aside after Polonius's speech on religious hypocrisy. This short speech foreshadows his anguished soliloquy in III, 3, when he tries in vain to pray for repentance. Ophelia believes that Hamlet's apparent madness is real, and, ironically, this allows her to rationalize his cruel treatment: "O, what a noble mind is here o'erthrown."

Soliloquy: The most famous speech in this scene and in the play as a whole is Hamlet's soliloquy: "To be, or not to be: that is the question. . . ." Typically, Hamlet applies his formidable intellectual powers to the analysis of a *question.* As he debates with himself the matter of suicide, he concludes that only fear of the unknown after death "makes us rather bear those ills we have/Than fly to others that we know not of." Unlike his soliloquy in Act I, Hamlet here makes no mention of suicide as sinful, perhaps signaling his increased anguish at the pain of his life.

Act III, Scene 2

Plot Synopsis

Hamlet learns from Polonius that the king and queen will attend the play-within-a-play, and he directs the players on how they should perform. Horatio enters, and Hamlet praises him as a true friend. He reveals that one scene of the play-within-a-play will present a striking parallel to the circumstances of Old Hamlet's death, and he urges Horatio to watch Claudius closely for any signs of guilt the king may betray.

The king and the queen enter with members of the court, Polonius, Ophelia, Rosencrantz, Guildenstern, and the players. Hamlet refuses to sit with his mother but rather reclines at Ophelia's feet where, following some ribald banter, he bursts out in grief when Ophelia reminds him four months have passed since his father's death.

The players preface the play-within-a-play with a dumb show. A Player Queen and Player King lovingly embrace. She then leaves him lying asleep on a bank of flowers. Another man enters, removes the Player King's crown, and pours poison into the sleeping king's ear. The murderer then woos the Player Queen with gifts.

The players then reenact the plot with dialogue. The Queen protests her undying love to the King, swearing that she would never remarry if he should die and leave her a widow. The King lies down to sleep. Hamlet tells Claudius that the title of the play is *The Mousetrap* and that it dramatizes the murder in Vienna of the Duke Gonzago by his nephew Lucianus. The play continues, with Lucianus pouring the poison in Gonzago's ears. At this point, Claudius rises and departs suddenly, calling for lights. All but Hamlet and Horatio also leave.

Hamlet, in a fever of excitement, triumphantly tells Horatio that Claudius has plainly revealed his guilt. Rosencrantz and Guildenstern enter to tell Hamlet that Claudius is fearfully angry and that Gertrude has sent for Hamlet, a request that is reinforced by Polonius. Left alone, Hamlet contemplates his anger

at his mother in a short soliloquy. He resolves to reproach her sharply in their upcoming interview but to do her no violence.

Literary Elements

Theme and Plot: In the opening section of the scene, Shakespeare directs our attention to Hamlet as actor and to the prominent theme of **acting,** or pretense, in the play as a whole. Hamlet's elaborate "stage directions" are a way of building suspense for the audience and also of characterizing Hamlet's inner state of suspense as he prepares this crucial test for Claudius. Hamlet knows that the test may fail. If not performed with just the right element of verisimilitude, the play-within-a-play may not provoke Claudius to betray his guilt visibly; on the other hand, if the performance is too obviously overdone, Claudius may easily see through it as a trap.

The play-within-a-play leads to the structural climax, or turning point, of *Hamlet:* the revelation that Claudius is indeed the murderer of Hamlet's father and that Hamlet must fulfill the Ghost's demands for revenge. It is significant that the play is enacted twice: once as a dumb show and once with dialogue. Also note the two titles for the production: *The Mousetrap* and *The Murder of Gonzago.* The first title is a thinly veiled reference to the play's function as a trap for Claudius.

Irony: In addition to the parallels between the stage action and the murder of Old Hamlet, Hamlet makes an ironic change in the script so that one critical detail is *not* parallel to what happened in real life: The murderer of Gonzago, Lucianus, is not the king's brother, but rather his *nephew.* Hamlet, of course, is Claudius's nephew; his objective may be to unnerve the king even further by foreshadowing Claudius's own death.

Allusion: Shakespeare may be indulging in a facetious, contemporary allusion when he has Polonius claim to have played Julius Caesar in a university production. Irrespective of an anachronism (Polonius presumably attended university many years previously), Elizabethan audiences would probably recall Shakespeare's own *Julius Caesar* (1599), played only two years or so before *Hamlet*. The reference is also an ironic, oblique foreshadowing of Polonius's own death by stabbing in III, 4. Note Hamlet's mocking puns on the words *Brutus, brute,* and *capital.*

Act III, Scene 3

Plot Synopsis

Shaken by the play-within-a-play, Claudius tells Rosencrantz and Guildenstern that he cannot afford to delay Hamlet's departure for England. The courtiers sycophantically comment on the importance of the king's safety. Polonius enters and tells the king that he will hide behind the curtain in Gertrude's chamber to spy on Hamlet. After Polonius exits, Claudius soliloquizes on his guilt. He knows he cannot truly pray for forgiveness because he is unwilling to relinquish the fruits of his crime: his murdered brother's throne and wife. Even so, he forces himself to kneel to beg heaven's forgiveness.

Hamlet enters and sees Claudius at his prayers. At first he resolves to kill the king. Then, he realizes that by killing the king while he is at prayer, Claudius's soul will go to heaven and Hamlet and the Ghost will be cheated of true revenge. As Hamlet leaves, Claudius rises, sadly remarking that he has been unable to repent.

Literary Elements

Plot: In this brief scene, Shakespeare advances the plot in at least two ways: Claudius is shown as so unnerved by the play-within-a-play that he determines to send Hamlet to England immediately, and Polonius—characteristically meddlesome—prepares to spy on Hamlet's interview with Gertrude.

Irony: The chief question that the scene poses is Hamlet's failure to capitalize on the chance to slay Claudius, now that he has proof of his uncle's guilt. Hamlet reasons that if he murders Claudius while the king is praying, the dead man's soul will go to heaven. This will have the ironic effect of cheating Hamlet and his father of vengeance. Such a result would be particularly galling because Claudius gave the old king no time to repent before he was murdered.

Then the final couplet of the scene provides a devastating stroke of dramatic irony. Claudius unwittingly reveals that Hamlet's delay was needless after all; though kneeling in prayer, the king has found himself unable to repent: "My words fly up, my thoughts remain below;/Words without thoughts never to heaven go."

Theme: The scene also shows how Hamlet's **thought** delays or checks **action** that would ensure **revenge.**

Act III, Scene 4

Plot Synopsis

In Gertrude's private chamber, Polonius urges the queen to scold Hamlet for his pranks. He hides behind the curtain. Hamlet enters, furiously reproaching his mother for her remarriage. Gertrude starts back, fearing violence, and cries for help. When Polonius echoes her cry from behind the curtain, Hamlet thrusts his sword through the draperies, killing the old man. Thinking that he may have killed the king, he lifts the curtain to find the body of Polonius, whom he calls a meddlesome fool. Turning to his mother, Hamlet passionately upbraids her for her remarriage. He compares Old Hamlet to the gods of classical myth and calls Claudius a foul, murdering villain. Gertrude sorrowfully admits that lust has corrupted her soul and begs Hamlet not to linger on her guilt. The Ghost of Hamlet's father appears and commands

Hamlet to carry out vengeance on Claudius but not to harm Gertrude. The queen, who cannot see the Ghost, concludes that now Hamlet is truly mad. Hamlet, however, assures her that he is sane and bids her atone for her sin by abstaining from Claudius's bed. He then warns her not to reveal that he is only pretending insanity, and she agrees.

Telling Gertrude that he must depart for England with Rosencrantz and Guildenstern, Hamlet hints darkly that he will repay their disloyalty. Then he leaves, dragging Polonius's body from the room.

Literary Elements

Style and Tone: Shakespeare establishes an angry, reproachful tone between Hamlet and Gertrude by employing *stichomythia,* alternating balanced exchanges delivered by two characters in a dispute or altercation. The artificiality of this style of dialogue consisting of brief lines swiftly gives way to terror as, fearing violence, Gertrude calls for help. Stichomythia, which originated in Greek drama, is often referred to

as "cut and thrust" dialogue, and is especially appropriate to Hamlet's actions in this scene.

Theme: The interview between Hamlet and Gertrude (**son and mother**) is dominated by the imagery of **corruption and disease.** To Elizabethans, Gertrude's remarriage to her brother-in-law would have seemed an incestuous union. Although it is clear that Gertrude was not an accomplice in Claudius's murder of her husband, it is also plain that the queen's besetting vice, or weakness, is lust. By indulging that weakness, she has helped to place Hamlet in a dangerous, if not impossible, position.

Plot: Hamlet's final speeches in this scene prepare for the next act in at least two ways. Foreseeing that Claudius will continue to probe his madness as real or feigned, he makes Gertrude promise not to reveal his sanity. Hamlet also indirectly foreshadows the deaths of Rosencrantz and Guildenstern, saying that he will "delve one yard below their mines/And blow them at the moon."

Act IV, Scene 1

Plot Synopsis

Claudius questions Gertrude on Hamlet's whereabouts and condition. Faithful to the promise she gave her son, Gertrude tells the king that Hamlet is "mad as the sea and wind when both contend/ Which is the mightier." She relates the circumstances of Polonius's death, and the king becomes even more alarmed, saying that Hamlet would have killed him if he had been in Gertrude's chamber. He declares that Hamlet must depart that very day, and he orders Rosencrantz and Guildenstern to find Polonius's body.

Literary Elements

Characterization: The queen is often described as a weak character with a will corrupted and paralyzed by lust. In this scene, however, she takes a considerable risk to protect Hamlet as she cooperates with his pretense of madness.

Figure of Speech: A notable feature of this brief scene is the use of similes. The first comparison, likening Hamlet's madness to the sea and the wind in a storm, is rather conventional. The next two similes are more interesting because they combine prominent motifs from the imagery in the play as a whole with considerable irony. In one simile, Claudius compares his previous gentle treatment of Hamlet to the behavior of a person who has neglected the proper medical treatment for a "foul disease." Here Shakespeare uses an ironic reverberation of the imagery of disease and corruption in the play, which is most often applied to Claudius himself. A few lines later, Gertrude uses a simile to compare Hamlet's madness to a vein of "pure ore," or gold, in a mine. This paradoxical figure of speech is also ironic because Hamlet has used his madness to conceal the "pure ore" of his own true nature.

Act IV, Scene 2

Plot Synopsis

Rosencrantz and Guildenstern attempt to find out from Hamlet where he has hidden the body of Polonius. Hamlet mocks them with insults, puns, and black humor. Continuing to "play mad," he runs offstage as if he were the target in a game of hide-and-seek.

Literary Elements

Figure of Speech: Hamlet uses an elaborate extended metaphor, mockingly comparing Rosencrantz to a "sponge" that soaks up the king's favor and is then squeezed dry.

Characterization: Once again, Hamlet is characterized as a master of verbal ingenuity; in the riddling statement on the "king" and the "body," Hamlet may be indirectly hinting at his ultimate revenge in the murder of Claudius.

Act IV, Scene 3

Claudius enters alone, remarking that he must treat Hamlet cautiously because of the prince's great popularity with the people. Rosencrantz enters and reports that he and Guildenstern have failed to discover Polonius's body. When Hamlet enters, along with Guildenstern and attendants, Claudius demands to know the whereabouts of Polonius's body, and after some mocking banter, Hamlet tells him that he has left it in the lobby. Claudius then tells Hamlet to prepare for an immediate departure. After everyone exits, Claudius reveals that the journey to England is in fact a death trap; sealed letters command the king of England to execute Hamlet immediately after his arrival.

Literary Elements

Plot: This brief scene advances the plot by dramatizing Hamlet's departure and by revealing Claudius's murderous intent in his letter to the king of England. At the same time, the scene increases suspense because Hamlet's aside shows that he is on his guard against the king's treachery.

Motif: Claudius sounds an important motif when he remarks that Hamlet's popularity with the multitude limits his freedom of action. Claudius will refer again to the people's love of Hamlet in his speech to Laertes in IV, 7.

Theme: The imagery of the scene reinforces the theme of disease and corruption. Hamlet puns on the decomposition of Polonius's body, and he significantly points out that even kings rot in the grave. Claudius uses the imagery of disease to refer to his own fears of Hamlet: "Diseases desperate grown/By desperate appliance are relieved,/Or not at all." Toward the end of the scene, Claudius boasts of his power to coerce the king of England to murder, referring to a recent "cicatrice," or scar, inflicted on England by the Danish sword. Hamlet is like a "hectic," or fever, raging in Claudius's blood: "Do it, England;/For like the hectic in my blood he rages,/And thou must cure me."

Act IV, Scene 4

Plot Synopsis

The scene shifts from the dark interior of the castle (where most of the play is set) to an open plain in Denmark, where the Norwegian general Fortinbras leads a large army toward combat in Poland. A captain explains to Hamlet the absurdity of the expedition, in which many will die fighting for an insignificant piece of land. Left alone, Hamlet compares himself to Fortinbras and reproaches himself in a soliloquy for delaying his vengeance and makes a definite decision to carry it out.

Literary Elements

Characterization: This scene marks the first appearance of Fortinbras, whom Claudius has characterized as aggressive and ambitious. Here his chief importance is as a decisive foil to Hamlet, who watches as the Norwegian army crosses Denmark to engage in a petty action in Poland. However gratuitous the military action of the Norwegians may prove, it is their capacity to act and risk their own death that impresses the prince.

Soliloquy and Theme: In Hamlet's last great soliloquy in the play, he makes it clear that he has compelled his **thoughts** of **revenge** to **action** and is determined to kill Claudius.

Act IV, Scene 5

Plot Synopsis

At the castle, Gertrude and Horatio are confronted with Ophelia's insanity, caused evidently by the shocks of Hamlet's rejection and Polonius's death. Claudius enters and observes Ophelia's pathetic and demented behavior. When Ophelia exits, Claudius tells Gertrude that Laertes has arrived from France, bent on revenge for his father's death. Rumors also abound that the people are ready to overthrow Claudius and make Laertes king of Denmark.

Laertes bursts in, demanding that Claudius defend himself against rumors charging the king with Polonius's death. Claudius calmly promises that he will reveal the identity of Laertes's true enemy, but before he can prove his innocence, Ophelia reenters to sing an incoherent lament for the dead, scattering flowers as if on a coffin.

Laertes is shocked by this display of his sister's madness. After Ophelia's exit, Claudius assures Laertes that he will explain all the circumstances of Polonius's death. The king says that he is ready to surrender his power if Laertes remains unconvinced.

Literary Elements

Characterization: Shakespeare characterizes Ophelia's madness convincingly by merging in the lyrics she sings the motifs of her father's death and her rejection by Hamlet. For example, her "true-love" is "dead and gone," like her father. Her pathetic lines when she exits, "Good night, sweet ladies/Good night," hint that she imagines herself at a court party or banquet.

Theme: The theme of **revenge** receives new emphasis with reports of insurrection against Claudius and with Laertes' excited entrance.

Foil: Laertes' situation, as a son determined to avenge his father's death, begins to cast him now as the principal foil, or contrasting character, to Hamlet. As the play progresses, it seems likely that Shakespeare stresses this relationship by punning on the word *foil,* in the sense of "contrast" and of "fencing sword." (Note the plot that Claudius contrives and explains to Laertes in IV, 7; and see V, 2, where Hamlet says, "I'll be your foil, Laertes.")

Act IV, Scene 6

Plot Synopsis

A sailor delivers a letter from Hamlet to Horatio. In the letter, Hamlet tells his friend to make sure that the seafarers deliver other messages to the king. He also reports that, two days after his departure from Denmark for England, his ship was attacked by pirates. Hamlet boarded the pirate ship just before the Danish vessel got clear. He thus became the pirates' sole prisoner. He reassures Horatio that the pirates have treated him well and hints that he has landed in Denmark. Finishing the letter, Horatio orders the messengers to lead him to Hamlet.

Literary Elements

Suspense: By leaving many questions unanswered, Hamlet's letter contributes to suspense, or uncertainty about what will happen next in the play. The audience is left to ponder these questions: What exactly happened in the rather implausible incident with the pirates, and how has Hamlet managed to return to Denmark? What are the marvelous events that Hamlet will relate to Horatio in person? What of Rosencrantz, Guildenstern, and Claudius's plot to have Hamlet murdered in England? They will have to wait until Hamlet's flashback early in V, 2 for the answers to some of these questions. Meanwhile, the audience remains in suspense about how Hamlet may accomplish his revenge on the king.

Act IV, Scene 7

Plot Synopsis

Claudius tells Laertes that Hamlet slew Polonius and is plotting against Claudius's life. When Laertes asks why Claudius has not punished Hamlet more severely, the king rationalizes his inaction by referring to Gertrude's love for her son and to Hamlet's great popularity with the people. Incited by Claudius, Laertes broods on revenge.

A messenger enters to deliver letters from Hamlet to Claudius and Gertrude. In his letters, Hamlet announces mysteriously that he has returned to Denmark and will appear in person on the following day at court.

Claudius reveals to Laertes a plot through which they can both be rid of Hamlet: The king will arrange a fencing match between Hamlet and Laertes, and Laertes will use a foil with a poisoned tip. As a backup, Claudius will prepare a poisoned drink to offer Hamlet if he fails to be wounded in the match.

Queen Gertrude enters, announcing that Ophelia has drowned, news that adds to Laertes' fury.

Literary Elements

In medias res: Shakespeare uses the convention of *in medias res* to start the scene: Laertes and Claudius appear in the middle of a conversation, and it is clear that the king has exploited the young man's thirst for revenge by filling him with half-truths about the death of Polonius. Laertes questions Claudius's failure to take stronger action against the prince; Claudius's answers, ironically, are more true than false.

Theme: The themes of **revenge** and **appearance versus reality** are especially dominant in this scene. Hamlet's planned murder at court must satisfy the claims of Laertes for revenge, but the death must appear accidental to avoid any trouble from Gertrude, whose love for Hamlet has been emphasized by the king earlier in the scene. Claudius takes special pains to flatter Laertes at length for his skill in fencing. His reference to Hamlet's "envenomed" envy of Laertes is probably an attempt by Claudius to spur on Laertes' hatred and desire for revenge, because Hamlet's "jealousy" has no independent support elsewhere in the play.

Act V, Scene 1

Plot Synopsis

In a graveyard near a church, two gravediggers discuss the imminent funeral of Ophelia and debate the theological issue of her burial, after a presumed suicide, in consecrated ground. Shakespeare's audience would be familiar with the church's denial of Christian burial rights to suicides on the grounds that they were guilty of a mortal sin. Hamlet and Horatio enter, and Hamlet muses on human mortality. When a gravedigger identifies a skull as belonging to Yorick, old Hamlet's court jester whom Hamlet knew when the prince was a child, Hamlet philosophizes on the inevitability of death as the common fate of humankind, rich and poor alike.

The court party enters, accompanying Ophelia's funeral procession. Laertes argues with one of the clergy about the proper extent of the funeral rites and then, crazed with grief, leaps into his sister's grave. Hamlet, too, leaps into the grave and grapples with Laertes, defiantly declaring that he had loved Ophelia. Claudius and Gertrude call him mad, and the king reminds Laertes in an aside to remember their plot.

Literary Elements

Theme: Relating to the themes of **corruption, disease,** and **death,** this scene functions as a graphic dramatization of Hamlet's final acceptance of the inevitability of death. The hero has longed for death in his emotional anguish; he has debated intellectually the question of suicide; he has killed Polonius with his sword and made macabre jokes about death; and he has been powerfully motivated by the sight of Fortinbras's soldiers, ready to risk their lives. Now, however, Hamlet encounters death physically: the rotting corpses in the graveyard, the skull of the jester Yorick, and the sight of Ophelia's body being borne to the grave impress on him the crude facts of human mortality. Hamlet's leaping into the grave to grapple with Laertes may be seen as symbolic of his readiness to avenge his father and to die.

The theme of **reality versus appearances** is addressed when Hamlet casts aside all disguise and pretense with his loud cry, "This is I,/Hamlet the Dane." There is now a clear sense that Hamlet has discovered the full range of his own identity.

Irony: Although Hamlet abandons his pretense of insanity, Claudius persists in calling Hamlet mad, (perhaps for the benefit of Laertes, the king's instrument of revenge); so does Gertrude, who has no way of apprehending Hamlet's new self-knowledge and who presumably remains faithful to her promise at the end of Act III to cooperate with his pretense of madness.

Act V, Scene 2

Plot Synopsis

Hamlet relates to Horatio what occurred aboard the ship: He discovered the commission from Claudius commanding his execution in England and substituted a new commission ordering that Rosencrantz and Guildenstern be executed.

Osric, a foppish young courtier, enters to tell Hamlet that Claudius has made a wager on the outcome of a fencing bout between Hamlet and Laertes.

Horatio urges Hamlet not to fight, saying he believes the prince will lose. However, Hamlet calmly reassures his friend, saying that he must accept his fate.

Claudius, Gertrude, Laertes, and the court party enter in preparation for the fencing bout. Hamlet reassures Laertes of his sincere friendship. Claudius places the cup of poisoned wine on the banquet table and, when Hamlet scores the first hit, offers the cup to Hamlet, who declines. When Hamlet scores a second hit, Gertrude picks up the poisoned wine and, ignoring Claudius's protests, drinks to Hamlet's health. On the third pass, Laertes wounds Hamlet with the poisoned foil. In the scuffle that follows, the foils are exchanged, and Hamlet wounds Laertes with the same poisoned foil. Gertrude falls, crying out that she has been poisoned. About to die, Laertes confesses to Hamlet the trick of the poisoned foil. In a fury, Hamlet strikes Claudius with the poisoned weapon and kills him.

After Laertes and Hamlet exchange forgiveness, Fortinbras enters, and Hamlet predicts that the young Norwegian will be elected king of Denmark. Horatio sadly blesses Hamlet as the prince dies. Fortinbras assumes command and orders a military funeral with honors for Hamlet.

Literary Elements

Theme: Perhaps the most important thematic aspect of this scene is the hero's philosophical acceptance of death. As he says to Horatio, "There's special providence in the fall of a sparrow. . . . the readiness is all."

Figure of Speech: Hamlet's use of acting metaphors in this scene is significant: "Ere I could make a prologue to my brains,/They had begun the play."

Throughout much of the action Hamlet has been forced to play a part; however, the time is soon to come when all pretense will be stripped away.

Plot and Theme: The fencing bout and its catastrophic outcome comprise the dramatic climax of the play. The strokes of chance or coincidence that serve to foil both stratagems of Claudius's plot are simply and naturally motivated: Gertrude drinks from the poisoned cup because she wants to cheer her son on with a toast, and Laertes inadvertently loses hold of his poisoned weapon in a scuffle with Hamlet. At the climactic moment of **revenge,** when Hamlet stabs Claudius, the prince puns sarcastically on the word *union*—referring to the pearl the king had hypocritically offered him as a prize as well as to Claudius's incestuous marriage with Gertrude.

The brief falling action and resolution of the play are notable: Fortinbras orders a military funeral for Hamlet, even though the hero seems more scholarly than soldierly. Perhaps, after the hero's suspicions of his own cowardice, the playwright wished to emphasize Hamlet's courage in facing and overcoming his doubts, in considering all points of view honestly and unflinchingly, and in finding at last the will to act.

Guided Reading

The Tragedy of Hamlet

The questions and comments that follow focus on the staging, characterization, and plot development of the play. They ask students for opinions and comments and are designed to help them think about and respond to the play as they read it. The questions correspond to specific lines in the play and are followed by answers or sample responses. You may want to use these questions and comments to help students who are having difficulty with the play; the annotations give students an opportunity to stop and catch up on the plot or understand the thinking of a particular character.

Act I, Scene 1

? Line 1. *The play opens with a dialogue between two sentinels holding watch outside Elsinore castle at midnight. What tone does the opening line set?*
ANSWER. The question "Who's there?" sets a tone of suspicion and tension.

? Line 13. *What can you infer about the midnight watch from Bernardo's speech?*
ANSWER. The midnight watch must be considered more dangerous than the others because more guards are required.

Line 14. You may want to make students aware that Horatio is Hamlet's college friend and confidant. Through Hamlet's conversations with Horatio, the audience is made aware of the hero's thoughts and feelings. Horatio also serves as a reasonable and pragmatic foil to the overly emotional Hamlet.

? Line 21. *What effect does this line have on the mood of the scene, and what questions does it raise?*
ANSWER. Reference to the appearance of "this thing" helps to reinforce a dark and eerie mood. The audience will wonder what it is that has been seen and what role the appearance of this thing will play in the story as it unfolds.

? Lines 42–45. *How would you have the actor deliver these lines?*
ANSWER. The lines might best be delivered quietly and urgently to express the guards' sense of fear mixed with curiosity about the Ghost's intent or purpose.

? Lines 79–107. *Summarize the information presented in this long and difficult speech. How does this information intensify the mood of the scene?*
ANSWER. The late King Hamlet of Denmark and the late King Fortinbras of Norway fought a duel, with specified portions of land going to the victor. King Hamlet killed Fortinbras and won a large amount of his land. Now, the Norwegian prince, named Fortinbras like his father, is raising a secret army to attack the Danes and reclaim the land his father lost, along with his life. (Young Fortinbras's situation mirrors Hamlet's in that his uncle assumed the throne following old King Fortinbras's death.) Students should understand that the threat of attack by the Norwegian army adds to the dark and fearful mood of the scene.

? Lines 126–138. *Why does Horatio advance toward the Ghost? How would you restate the questions Horatio asks the Ghost?*
ANSWER. Horatio advances toward the Ghost because he is concerned about the fate of his country. He suspects that the appearance of the ghost of the king must have some political or national significance. He asks the following questions: Is there anything I can do to ease your suffering? Do you know anything about Denmark's future? Have you left any buried treasure?

? Lines 149–155. *Why did the crowing cock force the Ghost to leave?*
ANSWER. The cock's crow signaled the approach of daybreak, and the Ghost can roam the earth only at night.

Act I, Scene 2

? Lines 1–16. *What is the purpose of the king's speech in these lines?*
ANSWER. The king is reminding members of his court that they agreed with his decision to marry Queen Gertrude, widow of the king's dead brother, even though the marriage quickly followed Old Hamlet's

48 | *The Tragedy of Hamlet*

Copyright © by Holt, Rinehart and Winston. All rights reserved.

death and despite the fact that a union between brother-in-law and sister-in-law was generally considered incestuous.

? Lines 17–25. *What topic does the king now address?*

ANSWER. The king discusses Fortinbras's secret army, pointing out that the Norwegian prince feels that Denmark's change of regime has made the country vulnerable to attack. Fortinbras is demanding the return of the lands lost by his father to Old Hamlet.

? Lines 26–39. *What are Cornelius and Voltemand asked to do, and why?*

ANSWER. The two courtiers are asked to deliver a message to the ailing king of Norway informing him of his nephew's intent to invade Denmark behind his uncle's back. Claudius hopes this action will prevent an invasion.

? Line 42. *How might Laertes respond physically as the king's attention turns toward him?*

ANSWER. He might approach the king and kneel before the throne.

? Lines 50–56. *What does Laertes ask of the king?*

ANSWER. He asks permission to return to Paris; he had traveled from France to Denmark to attend the king's coronation.

Line 58, Stage Directions. Polonius is usually portrayed as an elderly man, much too old to have such young children. He speaks in a high, reedy voice and is both wordy and obsequious.

? Line 65. *What does Hamlet's first speech reveal about his character?*

ANSWER. Hamlet's first speech is an aside, containing two puns: "A little more than kin" refers to his double relationship to Claudius as nephew and stepson; *kind* has two meanings—"kindly" and "natural." This use of puns reveals Hamlet as intelligent and quick-witted. It also shows that he is sensitive to the nuances of language, reflecting his emotional sensitivity. The aside also indicates Hamlet's feeling of disdain for Claudius.

Line 67. *Comment on Hamlet's pun on the word* sun.

ANSWER. On the one hand, Hamlet is saying he has been affected by spending too much time in the sun. On the other, he is expressing the grief of a son who feels unsheltered, having lost a father to death and now a mother to remarriage.

? Lines 76–86. *How does Shakespeare use this speech to introduce the theme of appearance versus reality?*

ANSWER. Hamlet says that the appearance of grief, such as heavy weeping, the wearing of black, and deep sighs, are ways to act out a show of grief but cannot express the real grief he carries within himself. He reveals his feeling of estrangement from his mother who seems unable to separate form from substance.

? Lines 87–112. *How would you summarize the king's speech?*

ANSWER. Hamlet has mourned too long, and because Hamlet is next in line for the throne, Claudius loves him as a son and wants Hamlet to look on him as a father.

? Lines 112–117. *What is contradictory about Claudius's request that Hamlet remain in Denmark?*

ANSWER. Claudius says he wants Hamlet to remain because he loves him and enjoys his presence. However, a loving father might prefer to see his son complete rather than interrupt his education.

Line 128, Staging Note. Left alone on stage, Hamlet begins the first of his soliloquies—speeches delivered to reveal the thoughts and feelings of an actor alone on the stage.

? Lines 129–134. *What mood is expressed by Hamlet's first thoughts?*

ANSWER. Hamlet expresses a mood of deep depression and despair with thoughts of suicide in the opening lines of this soliloquy.

? Line 135. *Throughout the play, Shakespeare employs images related to disease and* corruption. What might Hamlet be suggesting in his use of the image of the "unweeded garden" in this speech?

Answer. Hamlet is comparing an unweeded garden—"things rank and gross in nature"—to Claudius's unbridled appetite for power and for physical pleasures.

Lines 159–163, Stage Direction. After a pause, Horatio enters with Marcellus and Bernardo, but still lost in thought, Hamlet does not immediately recognize him. When Hamlet greets them, the three bow. Then Hamlet displays his feelings of camaraderie for Horatio by placing a hand on his shoulder.

Lines 187–188. *What can you tell about Hamlet's feelings for his father from these lines?*
Answer. Hamlet cared deeply for his father and is perhaps idealizing him. The image of his father remains with him in his thoughts.

Lines 247–254. *With what attitude might Hamlet address Horatio and the others in these lines?*
Answer. He probably addresses them with a conspiratorial tone in an attitude of excitement and urgency.

Lines 258–259. *It might interest students to know that most scenes in Shakespeare end in a rhyming couplet. Because there were no programs and because most audience members could not read signs marking the change of scene, this rhyming couplet served as an indicator that time had passed or that a new scene was about to begin.*

Act I, Scene 3

Lines 1–4. *How might Laertes demonstrate his feelings of love toward his sister as the scene opens?*
Answer. Laertes might say his lines while holding his sister's hand and looking at her in a loving way.

Lines 5–44. *What warning does Laertes give his sister prior to leaving for France?*
Answer. Laertes warns Ophelia about the dangers of falling in love, particularly when the object of her affec-

tion is the heir to the throne. He points out that such love can bring only heartache because royalty must defer to state demands (that is, marry royalty from another nation to assure peace between countries).

Line 44. *What does Laertes mean by this line?*
Answer. He warns Ophelia that youth is a dangerous time, that young people can feel strong desire without being aroused by another person.

Lines 45–51. *Summarize Ophelia's response to Laertes's warning.*
Answer. Ophelia accepts that the advice he gives is good but cautions him to avoid being hypocritical and to follow the advice himself.

Lines 58–80. *Some critics see this speech by Polonius as nothing but a string of clichés. What is your response to such criticism?*
Answer. Some students might suggest that their own parents have made similar speeches to them prior to a leave-taking, and so they might see Polonius's speech as that of a caring parent. Others might appreciate the speech in terms of its literary value—there is striking figurative language and both subtle and powerful rhythms apparent in the lines.

Lines 88–135. *What is Polonius's attitude regarding Ophelia's relationship with Hamlet? How does Ophelia respond?*
Answer. Polonius speaks harshly to Ophelia, objecting to her attachment to Hamlet. Ophelia draws within herself, responding minimally to her father's lecture.

Lines 105–129. *In this scene Polonius makes many references to money or financial transactions—tenders, sterling, brokers, investments, and bonds. What might these references reveal about his attitude toward his daughter?*
Answer. Polonius might see his daughter as property that he can use, in some way, to bolster his own fortunes.

Guided Reading (cont.)

The Tragedy of Hamlet

Act I, Scene 4

Lines 8–22. *Who does Hamlet criticize, and why?*
ANSWER. Hamlet criticizes Claudius for his excesses, particularly for his drinking. He claims that such excessive drinking makes Denmark look bad.

Line 24. *Claudius's "vicious mole of nature," or character flaw, will be revealed as the play progresses. However, the heroes in Shakespeare's tragedies also have character flaws. What might be Hamlet's tragic flaw?*
ANSWER. Hamlet's tragic flaw may be an inability to turn his thoughts and desires into action.

Lines 39–57. *What questions does Hamlet ask the Ghost?*
ANSWER. He wonders if this is an evil or angelic spirit and wants to know its intentions. He names it as his father's spirit and questions why it has decided to return. He asks what he should do.

Line 52. *What might the Ghost's arrival in "complete steel," or suit of armor, suggest?*
ANSWER. The Ghost is prepared to do battle over some unresolved conflict.

Line 90. *This is one of the most recognized lines from the play. What is the purpose of the line?*
ANSWER. The line reinforces the imagery of disease and corruption that occurs throughout the play. The reader will realize that the thing that is rotten is Claudius's character. The king's sinful behavior sets in motion a chain of corrupt acts that spread throughout his court.

Act I, Scene 5

Line 7. *What does the Ghost ask Hamlet to do? What effect does this request have on the plot?*
ANSWER. The Ghost charges Hamlet to avenge his murder. Achieving revenge becomes Hamlet's *action line,* or goal, and this is what creates suspense in the play.

Lines 9–14. *How can the Ghost be released from purgatory?*
ANSWER. He can be released only after his sins have been "burnt and purged away."

Lines 34–39, 46. *How do these lines reinforce the dominant theme of appearance versus reality?*
ANSWER. The Ghost explains that, even though it appeared he died from a serpent's sting, in reality he was murdered by Hamlet's uncle Claudius. His reference to the queen as "seeming-virtuous"—appearing virtuous when in fact she is not—also reinforces the theme.

Lines 53–57. *How do these lines connect to Marcellus's famous line at the end of Scene 4?*
ANSWER. These lines refer to the lustful relationship between Claudius and Gertrude in terms of garbage, creating an image that describes one thing that is rotten in Denmark.

Line 76. *What is the meaning of this line?*
ANSWER. Because King Hamlet was murdered in his sleep, without having a chance to confess his sins and without the sacraments or last rites, his sins were not forgiven.

Line 86. *What does the Ghost mean when, in reference to Gertrude, he says "Leave her to heaven"?*
ANSWER. He means that Hamlet should not harm his mother but rather leave her to be judged for her sins by God.

Lines 105–106. *What does Hamlet reveal in these lines?*
ANSWER. Hamlet's disgust at his mother's betrayal of his father appears to be stronger than his anger toward the murderer.

Lines 128–134. *How would you direct Hamlet to deliver these lines?*
ANSWER. Because the words make little sense, Hamlet's delivery should indicate a confused and agitated state.

Line 172. *What does Hamlet mean when he says he will put on an "antic disposition"?*
ANSWER. Apparently, Hamlet means that he will pretend madness to confuse the king, in hopes that an unsettled Claudius will reveal himself as the murderer.

Guided Reading *(cont.)*

The Tragedy of Hamlet

One of the key questions of the play from this point forward is that of Hamlet's mental state: Is he truly insane or is he simply feigning madness?

Act II, Scene 1

Line 1. *Knowing that Polonius likes to show his rank to inferiors, how do you think he might deliver this line?*
Answer. He would probably speak in a sharp and demanding way.

Lines 19–68. *What is the plan Polonius lays out for Reynaldo?*
Answer. Polonius wants Reynaldo to pretend, in his conversations with Laertes' associates in Paris, that Laertes is guilty of various youthful blunders. His bold assertions will force replies either in defense or in condemnation of the assertions. In this way, Polonius will learn how Laertes is behaving.

Line 27. *What can you infer about Reynaldo's thoughts from this line?*
Answer. Reynaldo is alarmed that Polonius is unconcerned about the damage he might do to Laertes' reputation.

Line 66. *How does this key line relate to the play so far?*
Answer. It is through indirection and subterfuge that Claudius has assumed the throne, married Hamlet's mother, and set the events of the plot into motion.
Lines 77–100. *Summarize what happens in Ophelia's private chamber.*
Answer. While Ophelia is sewing in her private chamber, Hamlet enters looking pale and disheveled and acting wild and distraught. He holds her wrists and looks into her eyes. Then, without taking his eyes from her face, he leaves the room.

Line 102. *What is the meaning of this line?*
Answer. Polonius feels that Ophelia has corroborated his theory about the cause of Hamlet's madness—his love for Ophelia.

Lines 113–120. *What does Polonius acknowledge in this brief moment of self-knowledge? What action does he then take?*
Answer. Polonius acknowledges that he has underestimated the depth of Hamlet's feeling for Ophelia, and his dogmatic opinion about the cause of Hamlet's madness may be wrong. He quickly dismisses that thought and, resuming his self-important attitude, goes off to share his findings with the king before Hamlet harms himself.

Act II, Scene 2

Line 3. *Using other people is a dominant plot device in the play. How might Claudius plan to use Rosencrantz and Guildenstern?*
Answer. Students might recognize that because Claudius is unsettled by Hamlet's "antic disposition," he will use Rosencrantz and Guildenstern to find out what is causing this behavior and how much Hamlet knows.

Lines 27–32. *How are Rosencrantz and Guildenstern characterized here?*
Answer. They seem obsequious and all too anxious to gain favor.

Lines 60–80. *What does Voltemand report to Claudius? What parallels can be drawn between the situation in Norway and that in Denmark?*
Answer. Voltemand reports that the King of Norway has persuaded Fortinbras to change his plans to invade Denmark. Instead, Fortinbras will use the army to invade Poland, and he requests safe passage through Denmark. Fortinbras has also been granted a large annual honorarium.

The political situations in Norway and Denmark are parallel: Each king, having inherited the throne from his late brother, now must deal with a wayward nephew.

Line 90. *What is ironic in this line?*
Answer. It is ironic that Polonius says "brevity is the soul of wit" when he is so long-winded and rambling in his speech.

52 *The Tragedy of Hamlet*

Copyright © by Holt, Rinehart and Winston. All rights reserved.

? **Line 129.** *Why does Claudius flatter Polonius?* **Answer.** Claudius knows that he must indulge the pompous and childish old man to get what he wants.

? **Line 173.** *What does Hamlet accomplish by feigning an "antic disposition"?*
Answer. Feigning an "antic disposition" allows Hamlet to ridicule Polonius without fear of reprisal. Calling Polonius a "fishmonger" (that is, a "pimp") also enables Hamlet to suggest that he knows the old man has sold out to Claudius and will use his own daughter for the king's purposes.

? **Lines 197–205.** *What is ironic about Hamlet's response?*
Answer. Hamlet is describing Polonius while reporting what is contained in the book he is supposedly reading.

? **Line 223.** *How would you compare Hamlet's demeanor now to that which he exhibited earlier?*
Answer. Hamlet seems to have dropped his "antic disposition" and is now acting normally.

? **Line 279.** *Why do you think Rosencrantz lies about his reason for returning to Elsinore?*
Answer. Rosencrantz wants to hide the fact that he and Guildenstern have been asked by the king and queen to spy on Hamlet.

Line 343. Innovation (here, meaning *disorder* or *disturbance*) refers to companies of boy actors that sprang up about 1600 to rival the established acting companies. This caused considerable hardship for the older actors, including those in Shakespeare's company. The term might also be a reference to the unsuccessful rebellion against Queen Elizabeth by the Earl of Essex in 1601. Some critics have suggested that Essex, a former favorite of the queen, may have been the model for Hamlet.

? **Line 380.** *How might Hamlet deliver this speech? Why do you think so?*
Answer. Because Hamlet has affection for the players and because he is clearly fascinated by the art of theater, he would probably deliver the speech with warmth and a feeling of camaraderie.

? **Line 464.** *What do Pyrrhus and Hamlet have in common?*
Answer. Each is seeking to avenge his father's death; both wear black clothes.

? **Line 510.** *Why might Polonius be so quick to find fault with the players and with their speeches?*
Answer. He probably thinks the players are beneath him socially, and he does not want to pay them positive attention.

? **Line 531.** *How does the language of the scene change at this point?*
Answer. The language returns to the elevated tone of blank verse.

? **Lines 615–620.** *What problem does Hamlet touch upon here?*
Answer. Hamlet addresses the question of whether the Ghost is indeed the spirit of his dead father or if it might be the devil trying to enlist him in sinful and destructive behavior.

Act III, Scene 1

? **Line 24.** *Why do you think King Claudius is pleased?*
Answer. He is anxious to have Hamlet return to acting normally, and Hamlet's interest in the play seems to indicate a move in that direction.

? **Lines 49–54.** *What does Claudius reveal in these lines?*
Answer. In this speech, Claudius gives the first indication of his guilt in the murder of Old Hamlet.

? **Line 56.** *What does Hamlet ask in this line, perhaps the most famous from the play?*
Answer. He is asking whether he should go on living or commit suicide.

? **Lines 97–99.** *Based on these lines, how would you describe Ophelia's feelings toward Hamlet?*
Answer. She seems still to love him as she recalls the sweetness with which he presented the gifts.

Lines 100–119. *Describe what is revealed in these lines.*

ANSWER. Although she acted on her father's orders to reject Hamlet, Ophelia now is forced to pretend that it was Hamlet who rejected her. Hamlet senses a trick and is angry because of Ophelia's seeming deception. He accuses her of leading him on, but his "I did love you once" is probably genuine.

Lines 137–153. *What does Hamlet think and feel at this point?*

ANSWER. He is now convinced that Ophelia is part of a plot to trap him, and he acts as if he cannot wait to be rid of her. He is unforgiving that Ophelia would allow herself to be used against him in this way.

Line 166–174. *What does Claudius now believe?*

ANSWER. He believes that Hamlet's "transformation" is not strictly the result of wounded love. Claudius plans to protect himself by sending Hamlet off to England.

Lines 180–182. *What does Polonius convey to Claudius here?*

ANSWER. Polonius still believes that Hamlet's madness was induced by Ophelia's rejection of his love.

Lines 192–193. *How might Claudius best deliver these lines?*

ANSWER. These lines might best be delivered with a tone of serious resolve.

Act III, Scene 2

Line 1. *What role is Hamlet assuming with the players?*

ANSWER. He is assuming the role of director, telling them how to deliver their lines.

Lines 61–93. *What aspects of Hamlet's personality are portrayed in these lines?*

ANSWER. His loyalty and gratitude are evident in this interchange with Horatio. The speech introduces two familiar Shakespearean devices: ideal friendship, in which great sacrifices are made, and the confidant

figure, a friend in whom the leading character confides so that the audience will understand more fully the hero's or heroine's thoughts.

Lines 97–100. *Why does Hamlet pretend to misunderstand Claudius?*

ANSWER. The pretended misunderstanding serves a dual purpose: Hamlet maintains the pose of madness, and he openly criticizes Claudius, referring to an environment filled with empty promises.

Line 104. *What is Hamlet's purpose in asking this question of Polonius?*

ANSWER. Hamlet wants to make Polonius look foolish. Like most fools, Polonius likes flattery.

Line 146. *Why do you think Claudius does not react when he sees the dumb show?*

ANSWER. Possible reasons include that (1) he is talking and not paying attention, (2) he senses a connection but chooses to ignore it, (3) he can't recognize the situation because of the stylized acting, or (4) because of where he was sitting, he couldn't see the show clearly.

Line 234. *How do you think Hamlet might deliver this line?*

ANSWER. He would probably speak the line with a mocking or sarcastic tone.

Line 247. *Why might the king ask this question?*
ANSWER. He is probably attempting to appear calm and unaffected by the play.

Line 281. *Claudius's saying "Give me some light! Away!" is often considered the turning point of the play. Why do you think this is so?*

ANSWER. This line marks the point at which the king has been caught in Hamlet's trap, and his running away is an indication of his guilt. Now that Hamlet has identified the murderer, the plot turns to resolving this conflict between Hamlet and the king.

Lines 377–386. *What is Hamlet's mood and tone as he delivers these lines?*

ANSWER. Hamlet's mood is one of anger and disgust. He probably delivers the lines with a sarcastic, resentful tone.

Lines 392–393, 395, 397, 401. *Why does Polonius agree so readily with Hamlet?*

ANSWER. Polonius thinks Hamlet is mad, and he is trying to humor him.

Lines 404–415. *What is Hamlet's mood as the scene ends?*

ANSWER. Hamlet seems to have a strong but sad resolve. He feels a son's love for his mother, and he regrets he must chastise her.

Act III, Scene 3

Lines 7–23. *What irony exists in these lines that form an extended metaphor describing the king as the center of a great wheel that touches all his people and suggesting the concept of the divine right of kings—that kings receive their right to rule from God, not from the people?*

ANSWER. The irony is that Claudius gained his throne through the killing of a king.

Lines 73–96. *Why does Hamlet not kill Claudius at this point?*

ANSWER. He does not want to kill Claudius while he is praying, because to do so would allow him to die in a state of grace. Hamlet recalls that Claudius killed Old Hamlet while he was sleeping, so the old king died without the benefit of last rites and was, therefore, not absolved of his sins.

Lines 97–98. *What does the king mean by these lines?*

ANSWER. He does not feel truly repentant or forgiven for the sin of killing his brother.

Act III, Scene 4

Line 6. *How do you think Hamlet should deliver his first line in this scene?*

ANSWER. Some critics think that this line should be spoken gently and sadly. Others think it is a line that should be delivered with strength and purpose.

Lines 9–15. *What do you notice about the structure of these lines?*

ANSWER. The repetition and quick exchange in this

dialogue is called *stichomythia*. It is frequently used in modern stage, film, and television dialogue.

Lines 29–30. *How does Hamlet respond to his mother's horror?*

ANSWER. He points out that what he has done is bad, but not as bad as murdering a king and then marrying the king's brother.

Lines 54–83. *Some stagings have Hamlet throw Gertrude to the floor and then crouch next to her as they examine portraits in a pair of lockets—Hamlet wearing one showing his father and Gertrude wearing one showing Claudius. Other stagings have Hamlet standing over his seated mother while he forces her to look at portraits on a wall. Which staging is truer to the spirit of the play, as you see it?*

ANSWER. Students should provide reasons to support their preference for one staging method over the other.

Lines 92–95. *What theme is reinforced in these lines.*

ANSWER. The theme of corruption, death, and disease is reinforced by Hamlet's description of his mother's physical relationship with Claudius. These lines echo Marcellus's line from Act I: "Something is rotten in the state of Denmark."

Lines 117–119. *Why do you think Gertrude is unable to see the Ghost?*

ANSWER. The Ghost's purposes during this visitation are related strictly to Hamlet: He reminds Hamlet not to harm his mother. More importantly, he appears so as to "whet thy almost blunted purpose" which is to avenge Old Hamlet's death by killing Claudius.

Lines 137–139. *What does Gertrude think is happening with Hamlet?*

ANSWER. She thinks he is mad and she is very concerned about his mental state.

Lines 189–200. *What do these lines suggest?*
ANSWER. They suggest that the very thing about the relationship between Hamlet and Gertrude that Polonius feared has occurred—that the bond of love that exists between mother and son has reestablished itself.

Guided Reading (cont.)

The Tragedy of Hamlet

Act IV, Scene 1

Lines 7–12. *In your opinion, does Gertrude truly think that Hamlet is mad? If not, why does she make the statement?*
ANSWER. Some critics have argued that Gertrude is trying to protect Hamlet by claiming that he is mad.

Line 13. *What does the king mean by this line?*
ANSWER. Claudius realizes that he might well have been killed by Hamlet instead of Polonius; he recognizes that Hamlet is now intent on revenge and mortally dangerous.

Lines 17–19. *What is the king's cause for concern?*
ANSWER. Claudius worries that the public will blame him for not having restrained the seemingly mad Hamlet.

Lines 24–28. *What is revealed about the queen and king in these lines?*
ANSWER. Gertrude realizes that Hamlet's mad acts have a noble cause; Claudius suspects that Gertrude might be more loyal to Hamlet than to him.

Act IV, Scene 2

Lines 17–23. *What does Hamlet express in this speech about the relationship between the king and Rosencrantz and Guildenstern?*
ANSWER. Hamlet points out that the two young men are foolish to bask in the attention they have received from the king because Claudius will have no use for them once he has gotten what he wants.

Line 32. *Why does Hamlet compare himself to a fox?*
ANSWER. Hamlet reminds the reader that, having revealed his intent by killing Polonius, he is now the quarry of the king.

Act IV, Scene 3

Line 14. *Why is Hamlet guarded?*
ANSWER. Rosencrantz and Guildenstern are holding Hamlet under guard until they learn what the

king wants them to do. Their allegiance is now clearly with the king.

Lines 34–38. *How would you restate this speech of Hamlet's?*
ANSWER. Hamlet is telling the king that if Polonius cannot be found in heaven, the king himself might look for him in hell. He goes on to say that, after a while, the smell of the decomposing body will lead the king to find Polonius in the lobby.

Line 52. *Why does Hamlet call Claudius "mother"?*
ANSWER. He is referring once again to the physical relationship between Claudius and Gertrude ("man and wife is one flesh") that he sees as incestuous. He knows that the reference, cloaked in madness, will add to the king's irritation.

Act IV, Scene 4

Line 27. *To what does Hamlet refer when he uses the term* imposthume?
ANSWER. Hamlet is referring to Denmark, which he sees as internally corrupt.

Lines 32–66. *What is Hamlet's attitude in this, his last great soliloquy?*
ANSWER. Hamlet is filled with self-recrimination. He sees everyone around him bent on action, and yet he does nothing. He feels he is no better than an animal.

Line 48. *Why might Hamlet refer to Fortinbras as a "delicate and tender prince"?*
ANSWER. Perhaps Hamlet is projecting these self-descriptors onto Fortinbras because the two have much in common, including the loss of a father-king and the loss of the throne to an uncle.

Act IV, Scene 5

Line 2. *Why might Ophelia be acting in this way?*
ANSWER. She has suffered the dual shocks of having Hamlet reject her in a cruel and unfeeling way and then of having Hamlet kill her father.

56 | *The Tragedy of Hamlet*

? Lines 17–20. *Why do you think Gertrude is feeling guilty?*

ANSWER. She probably feels that, by allowing Polonius to spy on her son, she is partly responsible for the old man's death. She also may be ashamed of having conspired to spy on her son and, perhaps, of marrying her dead husband's brother.

? Line 23. *To whom does Ophelia refer in this verse?*

ANSWER. She is singing about her dead father, Polonius.

? Lines 48–55. *To what do these two stanzas refer?*

ANSWER. Ophelia is singing about her unfulfilled love for Hamlet.

? Lines 65–66. *What do these lines suggest?*

ANSWER. These last two lines suggest a girl cast off by the young man she loves. Ophelia wrongly views her relationship with Hamlet this way.

? Lines 76–77. *To what does Claudius attribute Ophelia's madness?*

ANSWER. Claudius thinks Ophelia's madness springs solely from her father's death, refusing to believe that Ophelia's unfulfilled love for Hamlet is a factor.

? Lines 81–84. *Why might Claudius regret the haste with which they have buried Polonius?*

ANSWER. Such a hasty burial could cause questions among the populace about corruption and lack of control within the palace.

? Lines 122–125. *Why does Claudius not fear Laertes?*

ANSWER. Claudius believes that he is protected by the Divine Right of Kings.

? Lines 212–217. *Why is Laertes still not convinced of Claudius's sincerity?*

ANSWER. Laertes is suspicious because of the lack of details about his father's death and the unceremonious manner in which Polonius was quickly buried. He senses that Claudius might be trying to cover something up.

Act IV, Scene 6

? Line 10. *What is ironic about the sailor's use of the term* ambassador?

ANSWER. The sailor probably knows that Hamlet was not an ambassador but rather a troublesome prince whose king wanted him out of the way.

? Lines 21–23. *What good deed might Hamlet do for the pirates?*

ANSWER. The pirates expect that they will be pardoned if they are caught in Danish waters.

Act IV, Scene 7

? Lines 1–5. *What is Claudius trying to accomplish?*

ANSWER. Claudius is drawing Laertes into his confidence; he wants to use Laertes in his plans to get rid of Hamlet.

? Lines 9–24. *What two reasons does Claudius give for not having counterattacked Hamlet?*

ANSWER. Claudius says that he has not acted against Hamlet because Gertrude, whom Claudius claims to love, is devoted to her son and because Hamlet is popular with the public.

? Lines 49–50. *Why does Claudius suspect a trick, or "some abuse"?*

ANSWER. Claudius recognizes that his relationship with Hamlet has become something of a cat-and-mouse game, and he suspects Hamlet has a plan for his, Claudius's, downfall.

? Line 53. *Why does Claudius ask for Laertes' advice?*

ANSWER. Claudius is attempting to show that he values Laertes' opinion. In truth, Claudius is far from being at a loss.

? Lines 95–105. *What is Claudius's purpose here?* **ANSWER.** He is attempting to flatter Laertes by telling him that Hamlet is envious of Laertes' superior swordsmanship.

Lines 110–118. *How do these lines help reveal Claudius as a many-layered character rather than a one-dimensional villain?*

ANSWER. This beautifully expressed section dealing with the transient quality of love and the need to act when we have the will presents an intelligent, sensitive, and experienced side of Claudius's character.

Lines 134–135. *How does Claudius describe Hamlet?*

ANSWER. He says that Hamlet is an essentially trusting, somewhat naive, and open man; this makes him an easy target for Claudius's evil plan.

Lines 157–162. *What plan have Claudius and Laertes devised to kill Hamlet?*

ANSWER. Claudius and Laertes plan to engage Hamlet in a fencing contest wherein Laertes will use a sharpened foil that has been dipped in poison. Claudius will also be prepared to offer Hamlet a poisoned drink in the event their first plan fails.

Act V, Scene 1

Line 63. *How would you describe the mood of the scene to this point, and what helps to establish this mood?*

ANSWER. The mood, established by the gravediggers' banter, is one of rustic, somewhat morbid, humor.

Lines 69–70. *What aspect of Hamlet's personality is revealed here?*

ANSWER. Hamlet's tendency to be grimly serious, evident in earlier soliloquies and in speeches to his mother, is revealed again in this statement to the gravedigger.

Lines 128–135. *What wordplay do Hamlet and the First Clown enjoy here?*

ANSWER. The two enjoy their punning on the word *lie.*

Lines 155–170. *What information about Hamlet is revealed in these lines?*

ANSWER. The audience learns Hamlet's age, a surprising revelation because everything in the play thus far has indicated a man much younger than thirty. In a

way, Hamlet's age and his "lack of advancement" make considerable sense: If a man has chosen to remain a student until the age of thirty, he may not be ready to meet the demands of governing a nation.

Line 194. *How has the mood changed from the beginning of the scene?*

ANSWER. The mood in this second part of the scene is generally philosophical, with Hamlet musing on the transience of life.

Line 255. *What does Hamlet discover?*

ANSWER. He learns only now that Ophelia has died.

Lines 267–271. *What is Hamlet's intent with these lines?*

ANSWER. He is lashing out in consternation that his now-professed great love for Ophelia is not being accepted by the others.

Lines 287–297. *How do you think Hamlet would deliver these lines?*

ANSWER. Hamlet would probably speak with great sorrow, realizing suddenly that both he and Laertes have lost a loved one. He also realizes that he has lost a friend and gained an enemy in Laertes.

Act V, Scene 2

Lines 4–11. *How does Hamlet's behavior as he describes it here differ from the way he has acted in the past?*

ANSWER. He acted rashly, without giving too much thought to what he would do. He depended on what seemed to be a divine power guiding him. In the past, Hamlet has been self-critical about his tendency to think rather than act.

Lines 57–62. *How does Hamlet feel about the deaths of Rosencrantz and Guildenstern?*

ANSWER. Hamlet feels no guilt at their deaths. He has only contempt for them, although there is never any evidence that they knew of Claudius's plot. They were merely gullible nonentities used by "mighty opposites."

Lines 64–66. *What can you infer from the order in which Hamlet places the ways in which Claudius has wronged him?*

ANSWER. Hamlet is not particularly motivated by a desire for power or a need to assume the throne. He is driven to avenge the death of his father and what he sees as his mother's moral downfall.

Lines 93–106. *Why does Hamlet speak in such a confusing manner to Osric?*

ANSWER. Hamlet is making fun of Osric, causing the obsequious courtier to remove and replace his hat at Hamlet's whim.

Lines 210–212. *What does the queen want Hamlet to do?*

ANSWER. Gertrude wants Hamlet to apologize to Laertes for behaving rashly at Ophelia's burial. Hamlet sees the wisdom of this and agrees.

Lines 213–226. *Why does Horatio try to discourage Hamlet from dueling? Does Hamlet suspect a trap?*

ANSWER. Horatio speaks with concern as if he has a foreboding of Hamlet's danger. Hamlet is falsely confident because the odds are in his favor. This is the very thing, however, that makes Horatio suspicious. First, Claudius arranged a near-fatal sea journey, and now he has arranged a duel that Hamlet is all too tempted to agree to—there has to be a devious reason. Horatio's apprehension gives Hamlet pause. He knows that Horatio may well be right, but the cat-and-mouse game must play itself out. Hamlet becomes philosophical and resigned.

Lines 231–237. *How does Hamlet account for his behavior in this apology to Laertes?*

ANSWER. Hamlet tells Laertes that it was not Hamlet, but rather Hamlet's madness that killed Polonius and rejected Ophelia so cruelly.

Line 260. *In what way is Laertes Hamlet's foil, or contrasting character?*

ANSWER. Unlike Hamlet, who has struggled with his tendency to think too much and act too little, Laertes acts perhaps too quickly in avenging his father's death.

Line 301. *What does this aside reveal about Laertes' attitude?*

ANSWER. He is not convinced that he is doing the right thing by helping the king kill Hamlet.

Lines 349–363. *What does Hamlet express to Horatio as he prepares to die?*

ANSWER. Hamlet senses the justice of an assertive prince becoming the Danish king, as he himself was perhaps too contemplative. His "voice" or wish is that Fortinbras be king of both Norway and Denmark, thus bringing peace. The audience infers that he wishes Horatio to tell the unhappy story of Denmark throughout the world so that no nation will ever again allow itself to become so corrupt as Denmark has been.

Reader's Log: Model

Reading actively

In your reader's log you record your ideas, questions, comments, interpretations, guesses, predictions, reflections, challenges—any responses you have to the plays you are reading.

Keep your reader's log with you while you are reading. You can stop at any time to write. You may want to pause several times during your reading time to capture your thoughts while they are fresh in your mind, or you may want to read without interruption and write when you come to a stopping point such as the end of a scene or the end of the play.

Each entry you make in your reader's log should include the date, the title of the play you are reading, and the pages you have read since your last entry (pages _____ to _____).

Example

Sept. 21

<u>Fahrenheit 451</u>

pages 3 to 68

This book reminds me a lot of another book we read in class last year, <u>1984</u> by George Orwell. They're both books about the future—<u>1984</u> was written in the 1940s so it was the future then—a bad future where the government is very repressive and you can be arrested for what you think, say, or read. They're also both about a man and a woman who try to go against the system together. <u>Fahrenheit 451</u> is supposed to be about book censorship, but I don't think it's just about that—I think it's also about people losing their brain power by watching TV all the time and not thinking for themselves. <u>1984</u> did not have a very happy ending, and I have a feeling this book isn't going to either.

Exchanging ideas

Exchange reader's logs with a classmate and respond in writing to each other's most recent entries. (Your entries can be about the same play or different ones.) You might ask a question, make a comment, give your own opinion, recommend another play—in other words, discuss anything that's relevant to what you are reading.

Or: Ask your teacher, a family member, or a friend to read your most recent entries and write a reply to you in your reader's log.

Or: With your teacher's guidance, find an online pen pal in another town, state, or country and have a continuing play dialogue by e-mail.

| *The Tragedy of Hamlet*

Reader's Log: Starters

When I started reading this play, I thought . . .

I changed my mind about . . . because . . .

My favorite part of the play was . . .

My favorite character was . . . because . . .

I was surprised when . . .

I predict that . . .

I liked the way the playwright . . .

I didn't like . . . because . . .

This play reminded me of . . .

I would (wouldn't) recommend this play to a friend because . . .

This play made me feel . . .

This play made me think . . .

This play made me realize . . .

While I was reading I pictured . . . (Draw or write your response.)

The most important thing about this play is . . .

If I were (name of character), I would (wouldn't) have . . .

What happened in this play was very realistic (unrealistic) because . . .

My least favorite character was . . . because . . .

I admire (name of character) for . . .

One thing I've noticed about the playwright's style is . . .

If I could be any character in this play, I would be . . . because . . .

I agree (disagree) with the playwright about . . .

I think the title is a good (strange/misleading) choice because . . .

A better title for this play would be . . . because . . .

In my opinion, the most important word (sentence/paragraph) in this play is . . . because . . .

(Name of character) reminds me of myself because . . .

(Name of character) reminds me of somebody I know because . . .

If I could talk to (name of character), I would say . . .

When I finished this play, I still wondered . . .

This play was similar to (different from) other plays I've read because it . . .

This play was similar to (different from) other plays by this playwright because it . . .

I think the main thing the playwright was trying to say was . . .

This play was better (worse) than the movie version because . . .

(Event in play) reminded me of (something that happened to me) when . . .

Double-Entry Journal: Models

Responding to the text Draw a line down the middle of a page in your reader's log. On the left side, copy a meaningful passage from the play you're reading—perhaps a bit of dialogue, a description, or a character's thought. (Be sure to note the number of the page you copied it from—you or somebody else may want to find it later.) On the right side, write your response to the quotation. Why did you choose it? Did it puzzle you? confuse you? strike a chord? What does it mean to you?

Example

Quotation	Response
"It is a truth universally acknowledged, that a single man in possession of a good fortune must be in want of a wife." (page 1)	This is the first sentence of the book. When I first read it I thought the writer was serious— it seemed like something people might have believed when it was written. Soon I realized she was making fun of that attitude. I saw the movie <u>Pride and Prejudice</u>, but it didn't have a lot of funny parts, so I didn't expect the book to be funny at all. It is though, but not in an obvious way.

Creating a dialogue journal Draw a line down the middle of a page in your reader's log. On the left side, comment on the play you're reading—the plot so far, your opinion of the characters, or specifics about the style in which the play is written. On the right side of the page, your teacher or a classmate will provide a response to your comments. Together you create an ongoing dialogue about the play as you are reading it.

Example

Your Comment	Response
The Bennet girls really seem incredibly silly. They seem to care only about getting married to someone rich or going to balls. That is all their parents discuss, too. The one who isn't like that, Mary, isn't realistic either, though. And why doesn't anyone work?!	I wasn't really bothered by their discussion of marriage and balls. I expected it because I saw the movie <u>Emma</u>, and it was like this, too. What I don't understand is why the parents call each other "Mr." and "Mrs."—everything is so formal. I don't think women of that class were supposed to work back then. And people never <u>really</u> work on TV shows or in the movies or in other books, do they?

Name _____ Date _____

Group Discussion Log

Group members

....

....

....

....

....

Play discussed

Title: ....

Playwright: ....

Pages _____ to _____

Three interesting things said by members of the group

....

....

....

....

....

....

....

What we did well today as a group

....

....

....

....

What we could improve

....

....

....

....

Our next discussion will be on _____. **We will discuss pages** _____ **to** _____.

Making Meanings: Act I

First Thoughts

1. Do you believe that Hamlet is insane, or is his madness purely an act? Why do you think so?

Shaping Interpretations

2. Scene 1 offers little to establish or develop the **plot.** Why do you think it was included?

3. What is revealed in Act I about Hamlet's **character** and about his attitudes toward Claudius and Gertrude?

4. What does Claudius reveal about himself in Act I?

5. What does Hamlet mean by putting on an "antic disposition"? What do you think he hopes to accomplish?

6. Shakespeare addresses the **theme of disease and decay** through the use of **imagery.** Identify and discuss two such images.

7. What do Hamlet's two soliloquies (in Scenes 2 and 5) reveal about the changes in his nature?

8. From one angle the play is about the relationship of fathers and sons. Compare the relationships of Hamlet, Fortinbras, and Laertes to their fathers.

Extending the Text

9. How do you suppose Ophelia feels after listening to her brother and her father talk about her love life? Could a young woman today have Ophelia's problems? Explain.

Challenging the Text

10. What do you think of Hamlet's approach to his problems? Are there other actions he could take at this point to achieve his aims? Explain.

Writing Opportunity

Write a series of journal entries from Claudius's point of view.

READING CHECK

a. Describe the political situation in Denmark, as it is revealed in Scene 1.

b. Why is the ghost of Old Hamlet denied its eternal rest?

c. What delicate issues are at the top of Claudius's agenda for the meeting with his court?

d. Would the king rather have Hamlet stay at Elsinore or return to Wittenberg? Why?

e. How does Polonius tell Ophelia to behave toward Hamlet?

f. How did Old Hamlet die? What is the official account of his death?

g. What task does the father, from beyond the grave, set for Hamlet?

Name _____ Date _____

Reading Strategies: Act I

The Tragedy of Hamlet

Making Inferences

Watching or reading a play requires spectators or readers to draw inferences about characters based not only on what they say and do, but also on what other characters say about them. What is your impression of the characters introduced by Shakespeare in Act I?

Review the following characters and record your inferences about each one. The first one has been done for you.

Character	What the Character Says and Does What Others Say About the Character	What Can I Infer About the Character?
Hamlet	*Hamlet shows through his speech that he is quick-witted; adept at puns, double meanings, and irony. He reveals his despair through his soliloquies. Others describe his dark clothing and depressed mood.*	*Hamlet is sensitive, bright, passionate, and loyal to his father.*
Claudius		
Gertrude		
Polonius		
Laertes		
Ophelia		

FOLLOW-UP: Based on what you have inferred about these characters, how well do you think Denmark is being governed? Support your opinion with evidence from your chart or other evidence from the text.

Play Notes

Danzig

Act I, *The Tragedy of Hamlet*

Don't Try This at Home!

According to Danish custom, when the king proposed a toast, a cannon was fired. Shakespeare had firsthand knowledge of this clamorous custom. In 1603, a banquet was prepared for Shakespeare by the Danish king while aboard an English ship off the coast of Denmark. Another passenger recounted that six to ten cannon shots followed each toast, for a total of 160 blasts. In 1606, at another banquet, each toast offered by the king and his royal companions was followed by a drumroll and trumpet playing, as well as a cannon shot.

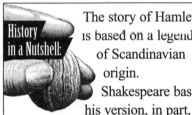

History in a Nutshell:

The story of Hamlet is based on a legend of Scandinavian origin.

Shakespeare bases his version, in part, on that of Saxo Grammaticus, a Danish historian, who wrote *Historia Danica* around 1200.

Shakespeare was probably acquainted with Denmark through the English actors, musicians, and composers who were employed by the Danish court toward the end of the sixteenth century. These entertainers included his colleagues William Kempe, George Bryan and Thomas Pope.

FOR YOUR READER'S LOG

If you could choose a modern-day setting for *Hamlet,* what place would you select and why?

MYTHS: NIOBE'S TEARS

Niobe of Greek legend married the Theban king Amphion and they had a number of children. Niobe was proud of her offspring and boasted that she had more and better children than the goddess Leto. This goddess told her sons to seek revenge, and the brothers Apollo and Artemis killed all but two of Niobe's children, causing her to weep endlessly.

As Hamlet notes, Gertrude, like Niobe, wept at the death of her husband. However, there was one major difference: When Niobe returned to her home, she was turned to stone on Mount Sypylus, where she continued to shed her tears.

BUST OF NIOBE

The Word PLACE

Shall We Danske?

Polonius inquires about Danskers in Paris, though at that time, the word actually used for Dane or Danish was *dansk.*

Dansker meant "of or from Danzig." *Dansker* also referred to "a person of or from Danzig." The Polish city of Danzig, or Gdansk, existed then as a free city under the protection of the Polish king and was a major port for English ships sailing in the Baltic Sea.

The words are so alike that maybe we should sit this danske out!

Choices: Act I

Building Your Portfolio

ART

Set Design

Working in a small group, create three-dimensional models or paintings of the stage sets for two scenes in Act I. Use materials such as construction paper, card, drawing paper, scissors, glue, markers, tempera paint, or modeling clay. Variety can be added through the use of found objects such as thread spools, rocks, cardboard tubes, plastic figures, lights, and glass beads. Your aim is to create settings that enhance the audience's appreciation of the action of the play. Display your creations in the classroom.

CREATIVE WRITING

Tattling Tabloids

Imagine that you are a reporter for a gossip magazine and you have been asked to cover the goings-on at Elsinore. Write a brief article describing the situation at the castle in a way that might appeal to tabloid readers. Consider the appearance of a ghost and the speedy remarriage of the widowed queen to her brother-in-law. Be sure to give your article an attention-getting headline.

PERFORMANCE

Select and Show a Scene

Working in a small a group, select a scene from Act I and prepare a performance. Choose a director and assign roles. Discuss how best to present the meaning and mood of your scene. You may decide to set the scene in another time period or location. Discuss and determine the types of costumes, if any, that you will use. Memorize the lines or read from the text, incorporating facial expressions and physical movement. Rehearse the scene until you feel comfortable with it, and then perform it for the class.

READING STRATEGIES

Summarizing

Draw a chart that shows a summary of what happens in Act I. Divide your chart into five sections, one for each scene. Remember that when you summarize, you focus on the main ideas. Make sure that you include all the important facts, but avoid adding too many details. Display your summary for the class.

Consider This . . .

"This above all: to thine ownself be true,/And it must follow, as the night the day,/Thou canst not then be false to any man." (I, 3, 78–80)

Restate these lines in your own words.

Writing Follow-up: Persuasion

Take a position either supporting or disagreeing with the above statement. Then, write four paragraphs that are intended to persuade others to your view. Use evidence from the text, history, current events, or your own experience to support your arguments.

Play Notes

Create an activity based on **Play Notes, Issue 1.** Here are two suggestions.

- Research Shakespeare's colleague William Kempe.
- Research other occasions that are celebrated with the firing of a cannon.

Vocabulary Worksheet

The Tragedy of Hamlet

Carefully read the definition and explanation of each word and the excerpt from
the play. Then, write a sentence of your own using the word. In each sentence,
try to include contextual clues that point to the word's meaning.

1. **assail** (ə sāl′) **v.** attack with arguments, questions, and so on; have a powerful effect on. ▲ Assail comes from the Latin *assilire*, meaning "to leap on."

   Sit down awhile, / And let us once again assail your ears, / That are so fortified against our story . . . (Scene 1, lines 30–32)

   Original sentence _____

   _____

2. **portentous** (pôr ten′təs) **adj.** that warns of evil; ominous. ▲ *Portentous* may also be used to mean "evoking awe or amazement."

   Well may it sort that this portentous figure / Comes armed through our watch, so like the King / That was and is the question of these wars. (Scene 1, lines 109–111)

   Original sentence _____

   _____

3. **privy** (priv′ē) **adj.** privately informed of. ▲ Privy comes from the Middle English by way of the Latin word *privatus*, meaning "private."

   If thou art privy to thy country's fate, / Which, happily, foreknowing may avoid, / O, speak! (Scene 1, lines 133–135)

   Original sentence _____

   _____

4. **invulnerable** (in vul′nər ə bəl) **adj.** that cannot be injured.

   For it is, as the air, invulnerable, / And our vain blows malicious mockery. (Scene 1, lines 145–146)

   Original sentence _____

   _____

5. **auspicious** (ôs pish′əs) **adj.** of good omen for the future; favoring or conducive to success. ▲ Auspicious comes from the Latin *auspicium*, meaning "omen."

   Therefore our sometime sister . . . / Have we, as 'twere with a defeated joy, / With an auspicious, and a dropping eye . . . /Taken to wife . . . (Scene 2, lines 8–14, excerpted)

   Original sentence _____

   _____

Vocabulary Worksheet *(cont.)*   Act I

The Tragedy of Hamlet

6. obstinate (äb´stə nət) *adj.* unyielding to reason or plea; stubborn. ▲ The word comes from the Latin *obstinare*, meaning "to stand against."

. . . But to persever / In obstinate condolement is a course / Of impious stubbornness. . . . (Scene 2, lines 92–94)

Original sentence _____

_____

7. impious (im´ pē əs) *adj.* lacking reverence or respect for God, a parent, or other authority.

. . . But to persever / In obstinate condolement is a course / Of impious stubbornness. . . . (Scene 2, lines 92–94)

Original sentence _____

_____

8. imminent (im´ ə nənt) *adj.* likely to happen soon; threatening. ▲ The word, which comes from the Latin *imminere*, meaning "to project over, threaten," is usually used to refer to expected danger or misfortune.

The canker galls the infants of the spring / Too oft before their buttons be disclosed, / And in the morn and liquid dew of youth / Contagious blastments are most imminent. (Scene 3, lines 39–42)

Original sentence _____

_____

9. precepts (prē´septs´) *n.* commandments or principles meant to serve as rules of conduct. ▲ *Precept* comes from the Latin *praecipere*, meaning "to take before, to order."

There—my blessing with thee! / And these few precepts in thy memory / Look thou character. Give thy thoughts no tongue, / Nor any unproportioned thought his act. (Scene 3, lines 57–60)

Original sentence _____

_____

10. pernicious (pər nish´ əs) *adj.* highly destructive; causing ruin. ▲ *Pernicious* comes from the Latin *perniciosus*, meaning "destructive." Here, Shakespeare may also be using the word in its now rare sense, meaning "wicked."

O most pernicious woman! / O villain, villain, smiling, damned villain! (Scene 5, lines 105–106)

Original sentence _____

_____

TEST   The Tragedy of Hamlet, Act I

A. Circle the letter of the answer that best completes the statement. *(20 points)*

1. The main action of *Hamlet* takes place in

    a. England   **c.** Denmark

    b. Norway   **d.** Germany

2. The play opens

    a. in a room inside the castle   **c.** on a plain near the castle

    b. on a platform outside the castle   **d.** in a small, church graveyard

3. Claudius is Hamlet's

    a. uncle and stepfather   **c.** friend and stepfather

    b. friend and confidant   **d.** cousin and friend

4. The Ghost claims to be

    a. Old Fortinbras   **c.** Julius Caesar

    b. Old Hamlet   **d.** Voltemand

5. The Ghost wants Hamlet to

    a. fight with Norway   **c.** take a message to Gertrude

    b. return to Germany   **d.** avenge his death

B. Answer each question using the lines provided. *(50 points)*

6. How would you describe the mood of the opening scene of the play?

_____

7. What helps to establish this mood?

_____

8. How does Claudius plan to avoid war with Norway?

_____

9. Before Hamlet hears anything from the Ghost, what are his feelings about the world in general and Denmark in particular?

_____

Name _____ Date _____

10. What similarities are there in the positions of Laertes and Hamlet in their families?

_____

_____

11. What is Ophelia's dilemma? How does she resolve it?

_____

_____

12. What helps Hamlet to overcome his fears and follow the Ghost?

_____

13. What does the Ghost charge Hamlet to do?

_____

14. Whom does the Ghost admonish Hamlet not to harm?

_____

15. In terms of the structure of the play, what is the overall purpose of Act I?

_____

C. Choose two of the following topics. Use your own paper to write one or two paragraphs about each topic you choose. *(30 points)*

a. Would Act I have been more or less effective had it opened with the enactment of the actual murder of the king? Explain your answer.

b. How does the message given Hamlet by the Ghost reinforce the expectancy and apprehension of the opening scene on the platform?

c. What qualities of Hamlet's character are revealed in Act I? Do you think these qualities will help or hinder him in his mission of revenge?

d. Hamlet's way to the throne has been usurped by Claudius. Does Hamlet indicate that he is ambitious for the throne? Support your answer.

First Thoughts

1. As you read Act II, which character impressed you most—either positively or negatively? Give reasons for your answer.

Shaping Interpretations

2. Cite examples of Hamlet's sense of humor in his exchanges with Rosencrantz and Guildenstern. In each instance, what is the joke?

3. Based on information provided in this act, what can you infer about Polonius's **character**?

4. What examples of madness does Hamlet exhibit? What might explain these acts?

5. What reasons can you give for Hamlet's rejection of Ophelia?

6. In what ways does Hamlet discover that "the time is out of joint"?

READING CHECK

a. Who is Reynaldo, and what is his job?

b. What does Ophelia report to her father concerning Hamlet's "antic disposition"?

c. How is Claudius's speech to Rosencrantz and Guildenstern like Polonius's speech to Reynaldo?

d. What trap does Polonius set to get Hamlet to reveal what may be on the young man's mind?

e. What is the source of Hamlet's "transformation," according to Polonius?

f. How does Hamlet propose to use the visiting actors in his conflict with Claudius?

Writing Opportunity

Setting it in modern-day society, rewrite Hamlet's rejection scene with Ophelia.

---

7. As the **plot** develops in Act II, several "fishing" parties have been organized: one by Claudius, one by Polonius, and one by Hamlet himself. Who is each man using, and what information or truth is he seeking to find out?

8. How do the actions in this act convey the **theme of life as theater**? Which characters are *not* involved in the make-believe? Which characters are wearing masks of one kind or another? What kind of act are they putting on?

Connecting with the Text

9. What do you think of Polonius using Reynaldo to spy on Laertes?

Extending the Text

10. The issue of social hierarchy—people belonging to certain classes, with little opportunity to move freely from one level to another through marriage or personal accomplishment—is an element standing in the way of a relationship between Hamlet and Ophelia. Think about the reasons for the American Colonies' break with England and the decision to have an elected president rather than a king or queen. How do these actions and beliefs reflect a different view of social classes?

Reading Strategies: Act II

The Tragedy of Hamlet

Summarizing

In Act II, Hamlet, Claudius, and Polonius make plans to spy on and entrap one of the other characters.

Summarize the plans for spying developed by the following characters. Identify the character under surveillance, and describe the reason for the plan. The first one has been done for you.

Plan and Reason for Plan

HAMLET
will spy on

CLAUDIUS

Plan *Hamlet hopes to prove that Claudius is guilty of Old Hamlet's murder by watching Claudius's reaction to* The Mousetrap. *The events of the play closely resemble the events of Old Hamlet's murder as it was described by the Ghost.*

Reason *Hamlet wants to ensure that the Ghost is telling the truth so that Hamlet can plot his revenge on his uncle.*

Plan and Reason for Plan

CLAUDIUS
will spy on

Plan

Reason

Plan and Reason for Plan

POLONIUS
will spy on

Plan

Reason

FOLLOW-UP: Which plan do you think will have the most influence on the outcome of the play? Give reasons to support your answer.

Play Notes

Act II, *The Tragedy of Hamlet*

ODYSSEUS

What They Read

In Ophelia's day, few people owned books, but many enjoyed listening to others reading aloud. Popular publications were cheap almanacs that became available around 1567, joke and riddle books, poetry and play books, and ballads. As many as 3,000 ballads were licensed between 1500 and 1700. After 1632, when it finally became legal to print the news in England, newspapers became popular. Chapbooks, the paperbacks of this period, contained stories of adventure and chivalry and often included female characters. "Long Meg," a strong and independent female character, was a well-known chapbook heroine. Most of the tales involving women, though, told of difficulties they faced when in love with a man of higher social status. "Patient Griselda," for example, possessed great virtue but remained loyal to her "abusive, aristocratic husband."

MYTHS: Hecuba

Hecuba became the second wife of the Trojan king Priam and had numerous children. Just before the birth of her second child, Paris, Hecuba dreamed that he would destroy the city of Troy. It was advised that Paris be killed; yet he was saved from death by exposure and accepted by the royal Trojan family.

When Troy was eventually destroyed, Hecuba became a slave of Odysseus. Later, after she discovered that King Polymestor had murdered one of her sons for his gold, she killed his infant sons and blinded him. Finally, she was turned into a fiery-eyed dog.

FOR YOUR READER'S LOG

What advice would you give to someone suffering from "melancholy" today?

Melancholy: A Sad Affliction

According to Robert Burton, author of *The Anatomy of Melancholy*, published in the mid-1600s, melancholy was characterized by sorrow, need, sickness, fear, grief, and passion. In Burton's day, this sickness had many definitions, such as "a bad and peevish disease, which makes men degenerate into beasts" and "a perpetual anguish of the soul, fastened on one thing."

Causes ranged from the supernatural and old age to love and one's parents. The most common cure for melancholy was blood-letting, usually done by applying leeches—blood-sucking worms—to the skin, accompanied by purification of the blood with certain medicinal remedies, such as sowthistle, carduus benedictus, and maidenhair.

INVESTIGATE

• *Were women taught to read in Ophelia's day?*

Robert Burton

Choices: Act II

Building Your Portfolio

RESEARCH/DISCUSSION

Just for Pun

A pun plays on the multiple meanings of a word or on two words that have different meanings but sound alike. Shakespeare made liberal use of puns in his plays. Often the puns are humorous, but other times they are used to reinforce an idea or a theme. With a partner, look through Acts I and II and locate at least four puns. Explain each pun's meaning, and tell the purpose of the pun in its particular context. Then see if you can make up a pun of your own.

ART

Spy Ring

In Act II various characters put into place plans to spy on or entrap other characters. Create a graphic design using connected circles to illustrate the inter-relationship of these plans. Begin with a circle in which you write the name or draw a picture to show who is doing the spying. Connect that circle with arrows to a second circle that shows the person spied on or plotted against. Be aware that some circles may have arrows pointing both toward them and away from them. Also, some characters may be spying on or plotting against more than one other character. As you work on your graphic design, consider how the use of shape and color can help you illustrate your ideas more effectively.

PERFORMANCE

Acting Out

With a partner, dramatize Hamlet's visit to Ophelia's room. It is not necessary to assume roles based on gender. Your dramatization will resemble pantomime because Ophelia reported no dialogue. Focus on exaggerating facial expressions and physical actions to express Hamlet's overwrought condition and

Ophelia's fearful response. After you have rehearsed your dramatization, perform it for the class.

CREATIVE WRITING

Journal Jottings

Compose a journal entry that Hamlet might have written after meeting with the acting troupe. The entry should indicate Hamlet's feelings about the troupe's arrival and his ideas about using the actors to serve his purposes. Be sure that the entry accurately reflects what is happening in the play.

Consider This . . .

"Brevity is the soul of wit." (Act II, Scene 2, 90)

Epigrams are short, witty statements that characterize or define. Explain the meaning of this epigram, and tell why it is or is not appropriate to its speaker.

Writing Follow-up: Persuasion _____

In two to three paragraphs, persuade your reader that the above epigram is true or not true. Support your arguments with examples from other stories, movies, TV shows, or personal experience.

Play Notes

Create an activity based on **Play Notes, Issue 2.** Here are three suggestions.

- Research the chapbooks of this period.
- Draw or paint a portrait of Hecuba in her human and canine forms.
- Research the education of women in Ophelia's day.

Vocabulary Worksheet
Act II

The Tragedy of Hamlet

Carefully read the definition and explanation of each word and the excerpt from the play. Then, write a sentence of your own using the word. In each sentence, try to include contextual clues that point to the word's meaning.

1. **piteous** (pit′ ē əs) **adj.** evoking or deserving pity or compassion.

   Pale as his shirt, his knees knocking each other, / And with a look so piteous in purport / As if he had been loosed out of hell / To speak of horrors—he comes before me. (Scene 1, lines 81–84)

   Original sentence _____

   _____

2. **perusal** (pə roo′ zəl) **n.** the act of examining in detail; scrutiny. ▲ Perusal comes from the Latin *per*, meaning "completely," and from the French *user,* meaning "to use up." The word is now often used to describe the act of going through something, such as a book, very casually.

   And, with his other hand thus o'er his brow, / He falls to such perusal of my face / As he would draw it. . . . (Scene 1, lines 89–91)

   Original sentence _____

   _____

3. **brevity** (brev′ ə tē) **n.** expression in a few words; shortness of time. ▲ The word comes from the Latin *brevitas*, meaning "short."

   Therefore, since brevity is the soul of wit, / And tediousness the limbs and outward flourishes, / I will be brief. . . . (Scene 2, lines 90–92)

   Original sentence _____

   _____

4. **satirical** (sə tir′ i kəl) **adj.** using ridicule, sarcasm, or irony to expose, attack, or deride vices, follies, etc. ▲ Here, Shakespeare may be using the word in its sense of "using good-natured ridicule to convey criticism."

   Slanders, sir; for the satirical rogue says here that old men have gray beards; that their faces are wrinkled; . . . (Scene 2, lines 197–199)

   Original sentence _____

   _____

5. **contrive** (kən trīv′) **v.** think up or plan; bring about.

   I will leave him, and suddenly contrive the means of meeting between him and my daughter. (Scene 2, lines 214–216)

   Original sentence _____

   _____

Vocabulary Worksheet *(cont.)*   Act II

6. **promontory** (präm´ən tôr´ ē) *n.* a high point of land or rock that juts out into a body of water; also used to refer to a bluff or a hill.

. . . and indeed, it goes so heavily with my disposition that this goodly frame, the earth, seems to me a sterile promontory; . . . (Scene 2, lines 307–309)

Original sentence _____

_____

7. **pestilent** (pes´tə lənt) *adj.* fatal; deadly. ▲ The word comes from the Middle English by way of the Latin *pestis*, meaning "plague."

. . . why, it appeareth no other thing to me than a foul and pestilent congregation of vapors. (Scene 2, lines 312–315)

Original sentence _____

_____

8. **pastoral** (pas´tər əl) *adj.* portraying rural life, usually in an idealized way. ▲ Here, Shakespeare is referring to a type of literature that deals with the lives and loves of shepherds in a highly artificial manner.

The best actors in the world, either for tragedy, comedy, history, pastoral . . . (Scene 2, lines 407–408)

Original sentence _____

_____

9. **affectation** (af´ek tā´ shən) *n.* artificial behavior engaged in to impress others; mannerism.

. . . there were no sallets in the lines to make the matter savory, nor no matter in the phrase that might indict the author of affectation. . . .(Scene 2, lines 452–455)

Original sentence _____

_____

10. **visage** (viz´ij) *n.* the face, especially the facial expression. ▲ *Visage* comes from the Latin *visus*, meaning "a look, a seeing."

Is it not monstrous that this player here, . . . / Could force his soul so to his own conceit / That, from her working, all his visage wanned, / Tears in his eyes . . . / . . . and his whole function suiting / With forms to his conceit? (Scene 2, lines 565–571, excerpted)

Original sentence _____

_____

TEST   The Tragedy of Hamlet, Act II

A. Circle the letter of the answer that best completes the statement. *(20 points)*

1. Act II opens

    a. on a platform outside the castle   **c.** in Polonius's house

    b. in the king's chambers   **d.** at Laertes' house in France

2. Polonius asks Reynaldo to spy on

    a. Laertes   **c.** Hamlet

    b. Ophelia   **d.** Claudius

3. When Hamlet enters Ophelia's room, he appears to be

    a. relaxed   **c.** happy

    b. distraught   **d.** exhausted

4. Rosencrantz and Guildenstern are

    a. Fortinbras's soldiers   **c.** Hamlet's childhood friends

    b. guards at Elsinore   **d.** Laertes' cousins

5. Voltemand reports from Norway that

    a. Fortinbras is trying to take over   **c.** Poland is about to attack
        the government   Fortinbras's army

    b. Fortinbras will not attack Denmark   **d.** the king has sent Fortinbras to live in France

B. Answer each question using the lines provided. *(50 points)*

6. How does Polonius react to Ophelia's story regarding Hamlet's visit to her room?

_____

7. What role do Rosencrantz and Guildenstern play in the king's plan?

_____

8. What trap does Polonius set for Hamlet?

_____

9. How, if any, has your opinion of Polonius changed since the beginning of the play?

_____

TEST   **The Tragedy of Hamlet, Act II** *(cont.)*

10. What forms does Hamlet's "antic disposition" take?

_____

11. After Hamlet has met the players, what does he want them to perform?

_____

12. What does Hamlet hope to accomplish by using the players in this way?

_____

13. What does Gertrude suggest is the cause of Hamlet's odd behavior?

_____

14. What does Claudius probably fear is the root of Hamlet's problem?

_____

15. What theme is strongly emphasized in the second half of this act?

_____

C. Choose two of the following topics. Use your own paper to write one or two paragraphs about each topic you choose. *(30 points)*

a. Describe how Claudius's intent in spying on Hamlet is different from Polonius's intent in learning about Laertes' activities.

b. Explain how Hamlet plans to "catch the conscience of the King." What reason does Hamlet give for being so cautious in taking revenge and so thorough in his search for evidence? Is his reason convincing?

c. An annoyed Gertrude tells Polonius, "More matter, with less art." What bothers her about the way Polonius presents his findings about Hamlet?

d. Which did you find more suspenseful, Act I or Act II? Why?

Making Meanings: Act III

First Thoughts

1. How has your opinion of Hamlet changed since the beginning of the play?

Shaping Interpretations

2. What qualities does Hamlet admire in Horatio? Compare Horatio to Hamlet's other "friends," Rosencrantz and Guildenstern.

3. Act III always marks the **turning point** in a Shakespearean tragedy, that is, the event or moment that determines the hero's fate. What would you say is the turning point in this act? Why is this moment so crucial to the **plot?**

4. Compare Hamlet's dialogues in Act III when he speaks with Ophelia and with Gertrude.

5. Some readers have found it odd that Hamlet talks of suicide in his famous soliloquy that begins "To be, or not to be . . . ", especially while his promise to avenge Old Hamlet's death remains unfulfilled. What reasons can you give for Hamlet's musings at this point in the play?

6. Describe Hamlet's state of mind as he moves from talking to himself to talking to Ophelia in Scene 1. Are there points at which he may be out of control? Explain.

7. In the scene with Gertrude, Hamlet is sometimes described as "overdoing it." Do you agree with this assessment? Why or why not? What evidence can you find that shows Gertrude knew nothing of Claudius's murder of Old Hamlet?

8. Predict why Hamlet's killing of Polonius is a costly mistake. How can it help his enemy, Claudius, and how might it affect the other **characters**?

Connecting with the Text

9. Ophelia is being used both by Claudius and Polonius to solve their problems with Hamlet. How might behavior such as this, by government officials, be reported and received today if it were leaked to the press?

Challenging the Text

10. Some critics emphasize the **theme of the relationship of thought to action,** claiming that Hamlet spends too much time thinking about his problems and planning ways to solve them. Do you think Hamlet's hesitations are believable? Explain.

Writing Opportunity

From Horatio's point of view, write a short description of his friend Hamlet.

READING CHECK

a. How is Ophelia being used by Claudius and Polonius to deal with their problem with Hamlet?

b. Describe Hamlet's ideas about death as expressed in the soliloquy beginning "To be, or not to be . . . ."

c. What decision does the king make after observing Hamlet and Ophelia?

d. Summarize the advice that Hamlet gives to the visiting actors.

e. Why does Hamlet not take his revenge during Claudius's prayer?

Reading Strategies: Act III

The Tragedy of Hamlet

Compare and Contrast

Analyzing similarities and differences between various elements of a literary work can help the reader better understand the plot, characters, and conflict.

Using details from Act III, compare and contrast each of the following. The first one has been done for you.

Rosencrantz and Guildenstern VERSUS Horatio as friends to Hamlet

Rosencrantz and Guildenstern: *They claim to be Hamlet's friends, but they conspire against him with Claudius. They are hypocritical flatterers who are interested in gaining the king's favor.*	**Horatio:** *He is a loyal and forthright friend to Hamlet. He is concerned about Hamlet's well-being and has proven that he is trustworthy.*

The murder of Old Hamlet VERSUS the play, *The Mousetrap*

Murder of Old Hamlet:	***The Mousetrap:***

Hamlet's opinion of his father VERSUS Hamlet's opinion of his mother

Hamlet's opinion of father:	**Hamlet's opinion of mother:**

The murder of Old Hamlet VERSUS the murder of Polonius

Murder of Old Hamlet:	**Murder of Polonius:**

FOLLOW-UP: Do each of the situations above help you understand character, plot, or conflict in the play? Explain how each element helps reveal the play's characters, plot, and/or conflicts.

Play Notes

Act III, *The Tragedy of Hamlet*

Feeling Empathy for Ophelia

In 1994, Dr. Mary Pipher published a book *Reviving Ophelia: Saving the Selves of Adolescent Girls*. In it she draws parallels between the circumstances of Ophelia and those of contemporary teenage girls.

Dr. Pipher's theory maintains that as she enters adolescence, Ophelia subdues her girlhood happiness to please others, namely Hamlet and her father. From her professional work, Dr. Pipher concludes that many adolescent girls suffer from a loss of self-esteem because of conflicting pressures. Depression, eating disorders, addictions, and suicide often result.

The book encourages a closer examination of cultural forces surrounding today's teenage girls in order to eradicate negative messages being sent to young women.

Sculpture of Ophelia

FOR YOUR READER'S LOG

If you were Ophelia, how would you feel at the end of Act III?

Going to the Chapel Again

Gertrude's quick remarriage violated the customary time between marriages for widows in England during Shakespeare's time. Between the late fifteenth and mid-seventeenth centuries, approximately thirty percent of all marriages were remarriages with widows waiting an average of two years before remarrying. Widows with young children were more likely to remarry.

The Word PLACE

Curious about these?

Bodkin: A short, pointed weapon.

Ecstasy: The state of being "beside oneself," thrown into a frenzy or a stupor, with anxiety, astonishment, fear, or passion.

Quietus: A discharge or release from life; death or that which brings death.

Frederick Warde as Hamlet

Awards for the Movies

- In his severely shortened 1948 movie version of the play, Laurence Olivier stars as Hamlet. The film received seven Academy Award nominations including Best Director, as well as four Academy Awards including Best Picture, and Best Actor (Olivier).
- Anthony Hopkins, in 1969, also played the unhappy prince.
- Fast-forward to the 1990s to see Mel Gibson's interpretation of *Hamlet*. Directed by Franco Zeffirelli, this version boasts a star-studded cast. The film received two Academy Award nominations, for Best Costume Design and Best Art Direction.
- Finally, in 1996, Kenneth Branagh both directed and starred in his four-hour rendition of *Hamlet*. This film, featuring many well-known actors, was nominated for four Academy Awards: Best Adapted Screenplay, Best Art Direction, Best Costume Design, and Best Original Dramatic Score.

INVESTIGATE

- *Under Danish custom, was a widow allowed to marry her brother-in-law, as Gertrude does?*

Choices: Act III

Building Your Portfolio

RESEARCH/PERFORMANCE

Play It Again, Ham

Find out the history of the recorder and present this information on a chart as the background for a musical presentation. Play several examples of music from the period or music that was created for *Hamlet*. You might like to compare and contrast your selections with modern pieces that deal with the same theme.

CREATIVE WRITING

An Obituary for Polonius

Imagine you are a writer for an Elsinore newspaper. Write an obituary for Polonius. Include personal information, such as a list of survivors and a description of what Polonius did for a living. You may want to include quotations that members of the court might have offered about Polonius. Include in the obituary the kinds of positive details you might share about someone who has died. Base your assessment of Polonius's life on his speeches and actions in the play to this point.

ART

To Be, or Not To Be

Create an abstract or nonrepresentational artwork that expresses Hamlet's mood and mental state as he delivers his famous "To be, or not to be . . ." soliloquy. As you plan your artwork, consider the mood and feeling expressed by various colors. For example, bright reds and yellows are generally considered to be hot, exciting colors, whereas cool greens and blues can be relaxing or, depending on the shade, somber. Also, consider that sharp lines and shapes create tense, anxious feelings, while curved and rounded lines and shapes are more soothing. Be creative with the medium you select—paints, markers, collage, or mixed-media. Give your artwork a title and display it in the classroom.

WRITING/PERFORMANCE

Stichomythia

Take another look at lines 10–14 in Scene 4, and then, in a small group, create a scene between Hamlet and another character in the play using stichomythia. Either perform the scene or record it on tape and play the recording for the class.

Consider This . . .

"Madness in great ones must not unwatched go." (Act III, Scene 1, line 193)

What is the meaning of this line spoken by Claudius to Polonius? Do you agree with the statement? Is it only "madness" in "great ones" that must be watched?

Writing Follow-up: Cause and Effect ▬

Give examples, either from history or from modern times, of the effects of the behavior of "great ones" on the course of events. How do we "watch" the "great ones" today?

Play Notes

Create an activity based on **Play Notes, Issue 3.** Here are two suggestions.

- Write a review of a film of *Hamlet*.
- Research the original or alternative meanings of the examples in The Word Place.

Vocabulary Worksheet

Act III

The Tragedy of Hamlet

Carefully read the definition and explanation of each word and the excerpt from the play. Then, write a sentence of your own using the word. In each sentence, try to include contextual clues that point to the word's meaning.

1. **turbulent** (tur´byoo lənt) *adj.* full of disorder; violently stirred up. ▲ *Turbulent* comes from the Latin *turbare*, meaning "to twist about."

   And can you, by no drift of circumstance, / Get from him why he puts on this confusion, / Grating so harshly all his days of quiet / With turbulent and dangerous lunacy? (Scene 1, lines 1–4)

   Original sentence _____

   _____

2. **insolence** (in´sə ləns) *n.* the quality of being boldly disrespectful in speech or conduct. ▲ Here, Shakespeare may be using the word in its now rare sense, meaning "the quality of being contemptuous or overbearing."

   For who would bear the whips and scorns of time, . . . / The insolence of office, and the spurns / That patient merit of the unworthy takes, . . . (Scene 1, lines 70–74, excerpted)

   Original sentence _____

   _____

3. **calumny** (kal´əm nē) *n.* a false statement meant to harm someone's reputation; slander. ▲ *Calumny* comes from the Latin *calumnia*, meaning "false accusation."

   If thou dost marry, I'll give thee this plague for thy dowry: be thou as chaste as ice, as pure as snow, thou shalt not escape calumny. (Scene 1, lines 137–139)

   Original sentence _____

   _____

4. **torrent** (tôr´ənt) *n.* a violent, rushing stream; a flood of words, mail, etc. ▲ *Torrent* comes from the Latin *torrens*, meaning "burning."

   . . . for in the very torrent, tempest, and (as I may say) whirlwind of passion, you must acquire and beget a temperance that may give it smoothness. (Scene 2, lines 6–9)

   Original sentence _____

   _____

Vocabulary Worksheet *(cont.)*   Act III

The Tragedy of Hamlet

5. temperance (tem´pər əns) *n.* the quality of being moderate or self-restrained in conduct. ▲ *Temperance* comes from the Latin *temperantia*, meaning "moderation, sobriety."

. . . for in the very torrent, tempest, and (as I may say) whirlwind of passion, you must acquire and beget a temperance that may give it smoothness. (Scene 2, lines 6–9)

Original sentence _____

_____

6. judicious (jo͞o dish´əs) *adj.* showing good judgment; wise and careful.

Now this overdone, or come tardy off, though it make the unskillful laugh, cannot but make the judicious grieve, . . . (Scene 2, lines 27–29)

Original sentence _____

_____

7. clemency (klem´ən sē) *n.* leniency or mercy, especially toward an offender or enemy; an act of mercy.

For us, and for our tragedy, / Here stooping to your clemency, / We beg your hearing patiently. (Scene 2, lines 159–161)

Original sentence _____

_____

8. extant (eks´tənt) *adj.* still in existence; not lost or destroyed. ▲ The word comes from the Latin *extans*, meaning "to stand out or forth."

The story is extant, and writ in choice Italian. (Scene 2, lines 274–275)

Original sentence _____

_____

9. primal (prī´məl) *adj.* first; original.

O, my offense is rank, it smells to heaven; / It hath the primal eldest curse upon't, / A brother's murder! . . . (Scene 3, lines 36–38)

Original sentence _____

_____

10. conjoined (kən joind´) *adj.* brought together; combined.

On him, on him! Look you how pale he glares! / His form and cause conjoined, preaching to stones, / Would make them capable. . . . (Scene 4, lines 126–128)

Original sentence _____

_____

TEST | The Tragedy of Hamlet, Act III

A. Circle the letter of the answer that best completes the statement. *(20 points)*

1. In Scene 1 when Hamlet meets Ophelia, he asks her to

    a. pray for him   **c.** leave at once

    b. sing a song   **d.** tell him a story

2. Claudius plots to

    a. send Ophelia to a nunnery   **c.** reunite Hamlet and Ophelia

    b. send Hamlet to England   **d.** murder Polonius

3. The players preface the play with

    a. recorder music   **c.** a poetry reading

    b. a discussion of the action   **d.** a dumb show

4. When Hamlet enters Claudius's room, Claudius is

    a. sleeping   **c.** eating

    b. praying   **d.** reading

5. While in Gertrude's room, Hamlet

    a. stabs Polonius   **c.** fights with Claudius

    b. begs Gertrude's forgiveness   **d.** steals the royal seal

B. Answer each question using the lines provided. *(50 points)*

6. How does Hamlet speak to Ophelia when he comes across her reading a book?

_____

7. How does Claudius's opinion of Hamlet's condition differ from Ophelia's opinion?

_____

8. What can you tell about Hamlet's opinion of Horatio by the way Hamlet speaks to him?

_____

9. Describe the dumb show.

_____

10. What does Claudius plan to do to rid himself of Hamlet?

_____

TEST   **The Tragedy of Hamlet, Act III** *(cont.)*

11. Why doesn't Hamlet kill Claudius when he finds him praying?

_____

12. What does Claudius learn about himself while at prayer?

_____

13. Whom does Hamlet think he is stabbing through the curtain, and whom has he actually stabbed?

_____

14. Which of Polonius's character traits brings about his death?

_____

15. What political advantage will Claudius probably gain from Hamlet's murder of Polonius?

_____

C. Choose two of the following topics. Use your own paper to write one or two paragraphs about each topic you choose. *(30 points)*

a. Many people consider that Act III, Scene 2 contains the turning point of the play. What event in the scene might mark the turning point? Explain why you think so.

b. In his famous "To be, or not to be" soliloquy, Hamlet contemplates suicide. What reasons can you give for his rejection of suicide?

c. What do you learn about Claudius from his speeches and asides in Act III?

d. Describe the moral and political position in which Hamlet finds himself as a result of Gertrude's marriage to Claudius.

The Tragedy of Hamlet

First Thoughts

1. Based on the events of this act, what effect do you think a commitment to revenge has on people?

Shaping Interpretations

2. Compare the mad scenes of Hamlet and Ophelia in Act IV. What do the scenes reveal about the nature of each **character** and his or her vulnerability?

3. How is the political situation changed by the death of Polonius and the removal of Hamlet from the scene?

4. How much does Horatio have to do in Act IV? Why is his part in the plot so small?

5. Based on Act IV Scene 4, describe Hamlet's feelings at this point about **the relationship of thought to action** and about the idea of honor.

READING CHECK

a. Why doesn't the king confront Hamlet directly after the death of Polonius?

b. How does Hamlet use humor as a kind of weapon when he faces Rosencrantz and Guildenstern?

c. What does Hamlet decide after his chance encounter with a captain in Fortinbras's army?

d. What is the subject of Ophelia's songs?

e. Who becomes Claudius's new ally in the plot against Hamlet?

f. Describe Ophelia's fate, as reported by Gertrude at the end of Act IV.

6. Consider Ophelia's thought, "We know what we are, but know not what we may be." Discuss how it relates to herself, to Hamlet, and to Gertrude.

7. Examine Hamlet's use of humor in his confrontation with the king in Scene 3. How much of Hamlet's jokes and puns could be considered as treason if he were not supposedly insane?

8. What problems exist in the play at the end of this act? How might they be resolved? Can the play end happily?

Connecting with the Text

9. Hamlet is self-critical, particularly regarding his inability to act decisively in avenging his father's death. He accuses himself "Of thinking too precisely on the event," continuing that "thought which, quartered, hath but one part wisdom / And ever three parts coward." Describe a situation, either from your own experience or from literature or popular culture, in which difficulties have arisen from thinking too much about a problem instead of acting decisively to solve it.

Extending the Text

10. List examples from literature, film, or television in which characters are motivated by a desire to seek revenge for some wrong they feel has been done to them or someone they love. What generally results from the acts of vengeance? What strategies are best to use if one is the target of an act of vengeance?

Writing Opportunity

Based on the events in Act IV, write an ending for the play.

Reading Strategies: Act IV

The Tragedy of Hamlet

Determining Cause and Effect

Determining cause and effect is a useful strategy for organizing the play's events.

Complete the following cause-and-effect chart about the events to this point in the play. The first one has been done for you.

CAUSE	EFFECT
Gertrude tells Claudius that Hamlet has killed Polonius.	*Claudius, out of fear for his life, decides to send Hamlet to England and have him killed.*
Hamlet watches Fortinbras's troops marching to invade a town in Poland.	
	Ophelia goes insane.
	Laertes returns to Denmark from France.
Hamlet's ship is attacked by pirates on its voyage to England.	
	Laertes agrees to help Claudius in a plot to kill Hamlet.

FOLLOW-UP: Based on the events in Act IV, how do you think the play will end?

_____

_____

Play Notes

Act IV, *The Tragedy of Hamlet*

What's in a Name?

The two longest names in *Hamlet* are those of Rosencrantz and Guildenstern. The names are quite aristocratic—the families are two of the most noble and prominent in Danish history.

Hamlet is an English name, but Shakespeare gave the other characters in the play names from a variety of nationalities. Laertes and Ophelia are Greek; Claudius, Cornelius, Marcellus, and Polonius are Latin or Neo-Latin; and Horatio and Barnardo are Italian. There are a few Danish names. Yorick may derive from Georg, the Danish form of George. Gertrude is both English and Danish, where it is Gertrud.

FOR YOUR READER'S LOG

What was Ophelia's message in the specific flowers she gave to Laertes, Gertrude, and King Claudius?

History in a Nutshell: *Away to Kronborg!*

Frederik II began construction of a castle at Elsinore in 1574 and it took eleven years to complete. Named Kronborg, which means "Crown Forest," this well-fortified castle overlooked the sea and became known for the detested taxes that the Danish government extracted from passing ships.

Kronborg Castle at Elsinore

More Than Just a Flower

Shakespeare cleverly incorporated plants and their traditional messages to convey various themes in his plays. Observe what Ophelia offers to Laertes, Gertrude, King Claudius, and to herself.

- **Rosemary,** an herb, was often carried at funerals perhaps because it symbolizes new life or resurrection. It also symbolizes constancy, fidelity, enduring love, devotion, and memory.
- **Pansy** symbolizes remembrance, romantic love, thought, and self-sacrifice. It is the flower emblem of Trinity Sunday because the original pansy contained three colors in one blossom. It is reputed to bring luck.
- **Fennel,** an herb, was well known for its medicinal value, reputed to cure anything from snake bites to obesity and eye infections. It was also believed to ward off witchcraft and bad spirits.
- **Columbine** is a symbol of infidelity and can bring bad luck.
- **Rue** symbolizes repentance. In medieval times, rue signified morals and mercy, and in Shakespeare's day, magic and witchcraft.

ROSEMARY

INVESTIGATE • *What is the origin or meaning of your first name or family name?*

Choices: Act IV

The Tragedy of Hamlet

Building Your Portfolio

ART

Complex Characters

Select one of the major characters from the play and create an artwork about that character. Combine a variety of images and materials in a way that expresses specific aspects of the character's personality. For example, in a collage about Hamlet, you might include a crown to represent his royalty, a balance scale to represent his difficulty with decisions, and so forth. You can create a collage of magazine pictures, a mixed-media collage of pictures and found objects, or a three-dimensional found-object sculpture.

CREATIVE WRITING

Elegy for Ophelia

Write an elegy (or poem of mourning) for Ophelia from Laertes' point of view. Reread the description of Ophelia's death to gather details to include in the elegy. As you develop ideas for your poem, consider the variety of feelings Laertes might be experiencing, including grief over the death of his sister and his father, as well as anger and hostility toward Hamlet, who killed Polonius and rejected Ophelia.

PERFORMANCE

Crazy About That Song

With a group, practice reading Ophelia's songs in a choral reading style. Vary voice pitches, volume, tempo, and tone to create the effect you desire. You may want to repeat key lines, use echoing words, or apply vocal sound effects to enhance your performance. When you feel comfortable with the quality of your choral reading, present it for the class.

READING STRATEGY

Make a Prediction

Have small groups discuss how they think the play will end. Encourage students to give reasons supporting their predictions. Have each group member write her or his predictions on a sheet of paper. Have the group reconvene after reading the last act to discuss how closely they predicted the outcome.

Consider This . . .

"So full of artless jealousy is guilt / It spills itself in fearing to be spilt." (Act IV, Scene 5, 19–20)

Restate this couplet in your own words.

Writing Follow-up: Cause and Effect _____

Can you think of examples from your own life or from literature that show the truth of this statement?

Play Notes

Create an activity based on **Play Notes, Issue 4.** Here are two suggestions.

- Make a three-dimensional model of Elsinore Castle.
- Create a chart of flowers and their meanings.

Vocabulary Worksheet

The Tragedy of Hamlet

**Carefully read the definition and explanation of each word and the excerpt from
the play. Then, write a sentence of your own using the word. In each sentence,
try to include contextual clues that point to the word's meaning.**

1. discord (dis´kôrd) *n.* lack of harmony; conflict.

O, come away! / My soul is full of discord and dismay. (Scene 1, lines 44–45)

Original sentence _____

_____

2. gleaned (glēnd) *v.* collected or found out gradually.

When he needs what you have gleaned, it is but squeezing you and, sponge, you shall be dry again. (Scene
2, lines 21–23)

Original sentence _____

_____

3. craven (krā´vən) *adj.* extremely cowardly. ▲ The word comes from the Latin *crepare,* meaning "to creak."

. . . Now, whether it be / Bestial oblivion, or some craven scruple /. . . I do not know / Why yet I live to say
"This thing's to do," . . . (Scene 4, lines 39–44, excerpted)

Original sentence _____

_____

4. exhort (eg zôrt´) *v.* urge strongly by advice or warning.

Examples gross as earth exhort me. (Scene 4, line 46)

Original sentence _____

_____

5. conjectures (kən jek´chərs) *n.* theories or predictions based on guesses. ▲ The word's original English
meaning was "to cast together omens in order to foretell the future."

'Twere good she were spoken with; for she may strew / Dangerous conjectures in ill-breeding minds. (Scene
5, lines 14–15)

Original sentence _____

_____

6. impetuous (im pech´ oo əs) *adj.* done suddenly, especially with little thought; reckless.

Save yourself, my lord: / The ocean, overpeering of his list, / Eats not the flats with more impetuous haste. . . . (Scene 5, lines 98–100)

Original sentence _____

_____

7. incensed (in senst´) *v.* made extremely angry; infuriated. ▲ The word comes from the Latin *incensus,* meaning "to set afire."

. . . Tell me, Laertes, / Why thou art thus incensed. (Scene 5, lines 125–126)

Original sentence _____

_____

8. ostentation (äs´tən tā´shən) *n.* showy display, especially one meant to attract admiration or envy; pretentiousness. ▲ The word comes from the Latin *ostentare,* meaning "to keep showing," and Shakespeare here may be using the word in its archaic sense, meaning "display."

His means of death, his obscure funeral— / No trophy, sword, nor hatchment o'er his bones, / No noble rite nor formal ostentation— / Cry to be heard, . . . (Scene 5, lines 213–216)

Original sentence _____

_____

9. conjunctive (kən juŋk´ tiv) *adj.* serving to bind together; connective.

She's so conjunctive to my life and soul / That, as the star moves not but in his sphere, / I could not but by her. . . . (Scene 7, lines 14–16)

Original sentence _____

_____

10. exploit (eks´ ploit´) *n.* a deed or act, especially a bold, daring, or heroic deed.

. . . I will work him / To an exploit now ripe in my device, / Under the which he shall not choose but fall, . . . (Scene 7, lines 63–65)

Original sentence _____

_____

Name _____ Date _____

A. Circle the letter of the answer that best completes the statement. *(20 points)*

1. When Claudius asks about Hamlet's mental condition, Gertrude replies that Hamlet is

    a. depressed   **c.** sane

    b. mad   **d.** improving

2. Claudius orders that Hamlet must leave for England

    a. within the week   **c.** that very day

    b. when the weather changes   **d.** after he is tried for Polonius's murder

3. Claudius remarks that he must treat Hamlet cautiously because Hamlet

    a. is popular with the people   **c.** has a nasty temper

    b. is in poor health   **d.** might one day be king

4. On the open plain, Hamlet speaks with

    a. Norwegian general Fortinbras   **c.** his friend Horatio

    b. one of Fortinbras's captains   **d.** Rosencrantz and Guildenstern

5. Laertes is shocked and dismayed when he sees

    a. Gertrude   **c.** Ophelia

    b. Hamlet   **d.** Claudius

B. Answer each question using the lines provided. *(50 points)*

6. Where did Hamlet hide Polonius's corpse?

_____

7. What has Claudius planned for Hamlet on his arrival in England?

_____

8. What is the destination of Fortinbras's army? What is their mission?

_____

9. What accusations does Laertes make toward Claudius? How does Claudius respond?

_____

10. What behaviors indicate Ophelia's madness?

_____

TEST ▪▪▪▪▪▪▪▪▪ The Tragedy of Hamlet, Act IV *(cont.)*

11. What threat does Laertes pose to Claudius's reign as king?

_____

12. What news is contained in Hamlet's letter to Horatio?

_____

13. What tricks does Claudius use to win Laertes over?

_____

14. What is Claudius's plan for getting rid of Hamlet?

_____

15. How does Ophelia's condition lead to her death?

_____

C. Choose two of the following topics. Use your own paper to write one or two paragraphs about each topic you choose. *(30 points)*

a. Why didn't Claudius provide an elaborate state funeral for Polonius? Do you think such a ceremony would be expected? Why or why not?

b. In Scene 4, in a soliloquy, Hamlet expresses shame. What is he ashamed of, and what has prompted these feelings of shame?

c. Compare Laertes' response to the news of his father's murder with Hamlet's first response at learning of Old Hamlet's murder. Consider the circumstances each young man finds himself in at the time he learns of the murder, as well as the reliability of the reports of each murder.

d. When Hamlet says "Frailty, thy name is woman" early in the play, he gives his appraisal of feminine nature. In your opinion, do the events of Acts III and IV support or dispute Hamlet's appraisal? Give reasons to support your answer.

Making Meanings: Act V

First Thoughts

1. What title would you give Act V?

Shaping Interpretations

2. What effect does the Gravedigger's scene have on the **tone** of the play at this point?

3. How do Hamlet's remarks to Horatio in Scene 2 (beginning "Our indiscretion sometimes serves us well, . . .") reflect significant changes in Hamlet's **character** and in his attitude toward life itself?

4. Based on his conversation with Horatio, what can you tell about Hamlet's feelings toward Laertes?

5. Compare Hamlet's ideas about life and death at the beginning of Act V, as expressed in his remarks about Yorick, and later, in his remarks to Horatio moments before the duel with Laertes. In what ways is his sense of resignation now religious?

6. How do you explain the queen's final actions in the duel scene?

7. Why do you suppose there are no soliloquies in Act V? How do we learn Hamlet's thoughts?

8. What is ironic about Fortinbras becoming the new head of government? Think about the report Horatio will give to Fortinbras. Explain some of the ironies Fortinbras will find in the stories of "accidental judgments" and of "purposes mistook / Fall'n on th' inventors' heads."

Connecting with the Text

9. What are your reactions to the outcome of the dueling match? Do you think the **plot** could have been resolved differently? Explain.

The Play as a Whole

10. C. S. Lewis wrote, "The subject of *Hamlet* is death." Do you agree with this statement of an overall **theme**? Support your answer with details from the text.

> **READING CHECK**
>
> **a.** What do the Gravediggers discuss as they go about their work?
>
> **b.** Why is Ophelia denied the complete rites of the church?
>
> **c.** Who is Yorick? How does Hamlet speak of him?
>
> **d.** How did Hamlet take care of Rosencrantz and Guildenstern?
>
> **e.** How does the king propose to rid himself of Hamlet?

> **Writing ▶ Opportunity**
>
> Imagine that you are Horatio, and compose a speech to deliver to Fortinbras some time after the end of the play.

Reading Strategies: Act V
::

The Tragedy of Hamlet

Organizing Information

Revenge tragedies often end with a violent fury as those seeking revenge attempt to fulfill their missions. Much activity usually occurs in the last act as the final conflicts are
resolved.

**Sort out the destinies of the characters below by recording what happens to
each of them. If a character dies, explain how. If a character survives, explain
what he or she will do in the future.**

At the Fencing Match Between Hamlet and Laertes . . .

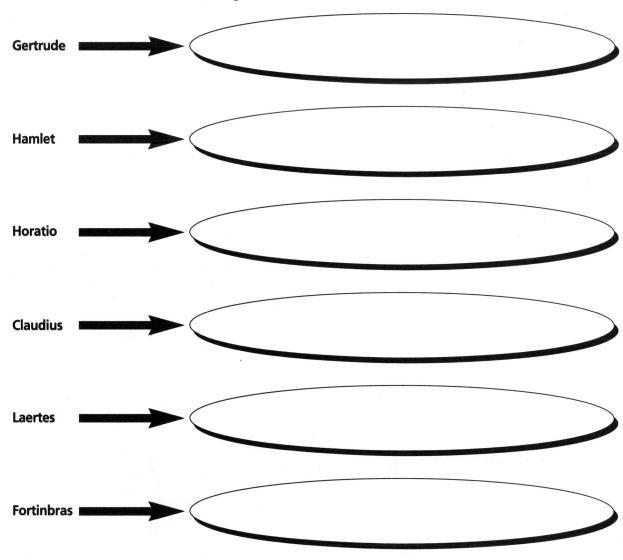

Gertrude ➡

Hamlet ➡

Horatio ➡

Claudius ➡

Laertes ➡

Fortinbras ➡

Who is alive at the end of the play? _____

**FOLLOW-UP: After reviewing your responses above, decide whether the play
could have had any other outcome. Present evidence to support your answer.**

Play Notes

Christian IV

Issue 5

Act V, *The Tragedy of Hamlet*

A Most Popular Duo

Rosencrantz and Guildenstern were famous before and after their appearance in Hamlet. In the time of Shakespeare, at least a few *Rosenkrantzes* and *Gyldenstjernes,* the Danish spellings of these aristrocratic family names, would have been present at any important occasion or ceremony of the Danish court. At the coronation of Christian IV in 1596, approximately 10 percent of the one hundred sixty noblemen in the procession were either Rosenkrantzes or Gyldenstjernes and two of the twenty councilors who assisted with the placing of the crown were Gyldenstjernes.

Several hundred years later, the two courtiers in *Hamlet* inspired playwright Tom Stoppard to write *Rosencrantz & Guildenstern Are Dead.* This play was first performed in 1967 by the National Theatre Company at the Old Vic Theatre in London. In it, the story of Hamlet is told from the point of view of the two courtiers who wander unconsciously and humorously towards their ultimate death.

In 1990, a film version of Stoppard's play was made. Directed by Stoppard and starring Richard Dreyfuss, Gary Oldman, and Tim Roth, this comedy, rated PG, won Best Picture at the Venice Film Festival in 1991.

Ouch! Watch That Blade!

Just try to get into a fencing class taught by Rocco Bonetti! The most popular fencing instructor in London in 1599, he first started teaching fencing in the late 1560s when fencing schools were proliferating around London.

In the first half of the sixteenth century, the practice of fencing with swords was being overshadowed by the use of the rapier and dagger. Henry VIII (1509–1547) was a big fan of this style, newly introduced from Italy.

It wasn't until the late sixteenth century that the duel of honor was introduced to England. A law in 1613 made it a crime to inflict death during a duel.

Choices: Act V

Building Your Portfolio

CREATIVE WRITING

Oh, Dear—uh—Diary

Imagine you are either Rosencrantz or Guildenstern. You have just learned that Hamlet has replaced his own condemnation letter with one condemning you, and you have only a short time to live. Write an entry in your diary that expresses your thoughts about what has happened and your feelings about what is to come.

ART

Movie Poster

Imagine you have been asked to design a poster for the newest *Hamlet* movie. Decide who will star in the movie, and then ask yourself these questions: Where and when will the movie be set? What scene or scenes will you highlight? How will you design the poster both to attract attention and to present information? Once you have organized your ideas, use colored markers, tempera paints, and a large sheet of poster board to create your movie poster. As you display your poster for the class, be prepared to answer questions explaining why you made certain choices.

PERFORMANCE

You've Got to See This!

With a group, decide on the details for a television version of *Hamlet*. Think about who will star in the play and how it will be presented—Will it be a miniseries? a movie of the week? a 13-week series? Then create an advertising campaign that will create viewer interest in the program. Once you have decided on what to include in the ad, assign parts and practice presenting the advertisement. Perform the ad live for the class, or videotape the ad and play the tape on your class television set.

READING STRATEGY

Hunting for Hints

With a group, reread the opening scene of Act I. Identify as many hints of action to come as you can find there. Discuss how such subtle foreshadowing effects your understanding and enjoyment of the play. Do you think these hints are fundamental to the play, or are they Shakespeare's way of playing a game by burying hints for clever observers to find?

Consider This . . .

"Let four captains / Bear Hamlet like a soldier to the stage; / For he was likely, had he been put on, / To have proved most royally;" (Act V, Scene 2, Lines 400–403)

Do you think that Hamlet, had he lived, would have been a great leader? Why or why not? Can you think of current examples or examples from history in which individuals who acted rashly or showed weakness have gone on to greatness in roles of leadership? Explain.

Writing Follow-up: Personal Reflection

Do you think *The Tragedy of Hamlet* could have turned out differently? Write two to four paragraphs explaining your position. Refer to the text as you state and support your ideas.

Play Notes

Create an activity based on **Play Notes, Issue 5.** Here are three suggestions.

- Research the modern Olympic sport of fencing.
- Research the history of dueling.
- Rosencrantz and Guildenstern discuss dueling: write the dialogue.

Name _____ Date _____

**Carefully read the definition and explanation of each word and the excerpt from
the play. Then, write a sentence of your own using the word. In each sentence,
try to include contextual clues that point to the word's meaning.**

1. **circumvent** (sʉr´kəm vent´) **vt.** go around; anticipate and evade or defeat by cleverness or deception. ▲
The word comes from the Latin *circumvenire,* meaning "to come around."

It might be the pate of a politician, which this ass now o'erreaches; one that would circumvent God, might
it not? (Scene 1, lines 82–84)

Original sentence _____

_____

2. **churlish** (chʉr´lish) **adj.** surly and ill-bred; selfish. ▲ The word comes from the Old English *ceorl,* meaning
"peasant, common person."

I tell thee, churlish priest, / A minist'ring angel shall my sister be / When thou liest howling. (Scene 1, lines
253–255)

Original sentence _____

_____

3. **diligence** (dil´ə jəns) **n.** painstaking attention to a task; careful effort. ▲ The word comes from the Latin
diligere, meaning "to select." Here, Shakespeare seems to be using the word in its obsolete sense to mean
"speed."

I will receive it, sir, with all diligence of spirit. (Scene 2, lines 92–93)

Original sentence _____

_____

4. **perdition** (pər dish´ən) **n.** eternal damnation. ▲ Here, Shakespeare is using the word in its archaic sense to
mean "loss or diminishment."

Sir, his definement suffers no perdition in you, . . . (Scene 2, lines 114–115)

Original sentence _____

_____

5. **verity** (ver´ə tē) **n.** truth; reality. ▲ The word comes from the Latin *veritas,* meaning "truth."

But, in the verity of extolment, I take him to be a soul of great article, . . . (Scene 2, lines 117–119)

Original sentence _____

_____

Vocabulary Worksheet *(cont.)* Act V

The Tragedy of Hamlet

6. edified (ed′i fīd) *vt.* instructed and improved; enlightened.

I knew you must be edified by the margent ere you had done. (Scene 2, lines 158–159)

Original sentence _____

_____

7. germane (jər mān′) *adj.* relevant to the matter at hand; to the point.

The phrase would be more germane to the matter if we could carry cannon by our sides. (Scene 2, lines 161–162)

Original sentence _____

_____

8. augury (ô′gyo͞o rē) *n.* foretelling the future by means of omens; an omen.

Not a whit, we defy augury. There's a special providence in the fall of a sparrow. (Scene 2, lines 224–225)

Original sentence _____

_____

9. palpable (pal′pə bəl) *adj.* that can be touched or felt; definite. ▲ The word comes from the Latin *palpare*, meaning "to touch."

A hit, a very palpable hit. (Scene 2, line 286)

Original sentence _____

_____

10. felicity (fə lis′i tē) *n.* happiness; joy.

If thou didst ever hold me in thy heart, / Absent thee from felicity awhile, / And in this harsh world draw thy breath in pain, / To tell my story. (Scene 2, lines 351–354)

Original sentence _____

_____

Name _____ Date _____

TEST   The Tragedy of Hamlet, Act V

A. Circle the letter of the answer that best completes the statement. *(20 points)*

1. The Clowns are employed as

    a. court jesters   **c.** soldiers

    b. gravediggers   **d.** gardeners

2. Hamlet recalls Yorick as

    a. his mother's brother   **c.** a court jester

    b. an aging courtier   **d.** a brave soldier

3. At the funeral, Hamlet and Laertes fight when

    a. Hamlet says cruel things about Ophelia   **c.** Hamlet insists on reading a poem

    b. Hamlet joins Laertes by leaping into the grave   **d.** Claudius urges Laertes to strike Hamlet

4. Gertrude's death is caused by

    a. a broken heart   **c.** a drink of poisoned wine

    b. a scratch with the poisoned foil   **d.** an attack by Fortinbras's soldiers

5. After Claudius dies, the Danish crown is bestowed upon

    a. Hamlet   **c.** Horatio

    b. Fortinbras   **d.** Laertes

B. Answer each question using the lines provided. *(50 Points)*

6. Why is Ophelia denied full burial rites?

_____

7. How does Hamlet's behavior at the burial site play directly into Claudius's plan?

_____

8. How did Hamlet rid himself of Rosencrantz and Guildenstern?

_____

9. What does the queen ask of Hamlet before his fight with Laertes?

_____

10. Describe the king's bet.

_____

Name _____ Date _____

TEST **The Tragedy of Hamlet, Act V** *(cont.)*

11. When does the king first offer the poisoned cup of wine to Hamlet?

12. How do Laertes, Claudius, Gertrude, and Hamlet die?

13. As Hamlet is dying, what does he ask of Horatio?

14. What news do the English ambassadors bring?

15. In what ways does the final scene cure Denmark's "illness"?

C. Choose two of the following topics. Use your own paper to write one or two paragraphs about each topic you choose. *(30 points)*

a. Describe the comic episode included in Scene 1. Why do you think Shakespeare would want to add this much humor to Act V?

b. Do you think Gertrude was aware that the wine was poisoned? Why or why not? How does her action in drinking the poisoned wine irrevocably change the course of action?

c. Discuss the main variations Shakespeare plays on the theme of love and loyalty, with reference to Hamlet, Ophelia, Gertrude, Claudius, and Horatio. Which attitudes seem to you most desirable? Which seem most objectionable?

d. What is your opinion of *Hamlet?* Would you recommend it to others? Why or why not?

Name _____ Date _____

Play Review

The Tragedy of Hamlet

MAJOR CHARACTERS

Use the chart below to keep track of the characters in this play. Each time you
come across a new character, write the character's name and the number of
the page on which the character first appears. Then, jot down a brief description. Add information about the characters as you read. Put a star next
to the name of each main character.

NAME OF CHARACTER	DESCRIPTION

FOLLOW-UP: A *dynamic character* changes in some important way as a result
of the story's action. In a paragraph, trace the transformation of one dynamic
character from the time the character is introduced through the conclusion of
the play.

Play Review (cont.)

The Tragedy of Hamlet

SETTING

Time ....

Most important place(s) ....

....

One effect of setting on plot, theme, or character ....

....

....

PLOT

List key events from the play.

- ....   • ....

- ....   • ....

- ....   • ....

Use your list to identify the plot elements below. Add other events as necessary.

Major conflict / problem ....

....

Turning point / climax ....

....

Resolution / denouement ....

....

MAJOR THEMES

- ....

- ....

- ....

Name _____ Date _____

Literary Elements Worksheet 1

The Tragedy of Hamlet

Conflict

Conflict is the struggle or clash between opposing characters, forces, or emotions in a work of literature. In an external conflict, a character struggles with an *outside* force; an internal conflict is a struggle between opposing emotions or ideas *within* a character.

Describe the conflict that exists between each of the following. The first one has been done for you.

CONFLICT

Denmark → *External: Old Hamlet, the late King of Denmark, killed young Fortinbras's father and gained Norwegian territory. Fortinbras has organized an army to take back the lost land and, in the process, avenge his father's death.* ← **Young Fortinbras**

Hamlet → _____ ← **Claudius**

Hamlet → _____ ← **Gertrude**

Hamlet → _____ ← **Hamlet**

FOLLOW-UP: Do you think Hamlet has more trouble overcoming his external or his internal conflicts? Explain your answer.

Name _____ Date _____

Literary Elements Worksheet 2

Theme

Theme is a central idea or insight of a work of literature. One theme in *Hamlet* is appearance versus reality—things, and people, are not always what they seem.

Describe how the theme of appearance versus reality is conveyed by a situation involving the following sets of characters. The first one has been done for you.

	Appearance	**Reality**
Hamlet with Polonius	Hamlet uses nonsensical language and appears mentally disordered in his exchange with Polonius.	Hamlet is merely acting insane.
Rosencrantz and Guildenstern with Hamlet		
Claudius and Gertrude speak to Rosencrantz and Guildenstern about Hamlet		
Hamlet with Ophelia		

FOLLOW-UP: When is acting—pretending to be something you are not—a positive, neutral, or negative activity in the play? Explain your answer.

Literary Elements Worksheet 3

The Tragedy of Hamlet

Irony

Dramatic irony occurs when the audience or reader knows something that a character in the play does not.

In the boxes below, explain the dramatic irony in the given dialogue. The first one has been done for you.

Polonius: We are oft to blame in this, / 'Tis too much proved, that with devotion's visage / And pious action we do sugar o'er / The devil himself. **King [Claudius]:** *[Aside.]* O, 'tis too true! (Act III, Scene 1, lines 46–49)	**Irony:** *Polonius does not realize (but the audience recognizes) that his words describe Claudius, who uses devotion to Hamlet and other "pious" actions to conceal his murder of Old Hamlet and his desire to kill Hamlet.*
Hamlet to Claudius in reference to the play, *The Mousetrap:* 'Tis a knavish piece of work; but what o'that? Your Majesty, and we that have free souls, it touches us not. (Act III, Scene 2, lines 251–253)	**Irony:**
Hamlet says to himself as he hesitates to kill Claudius while the King is praying: Now I might do it pat, now he is praying . . . /A villain kills my father; and for that, / I his sole son, do this same villain send / To heaven. [T]his is . . . not revenge! (Act III, Scene 3, lines 73–79)	**Irony:**
Rising from prayer, Claudius says: My words fly up, my thoughts remain below; / Words without thoughts never to heaven go. (Act III, Scene 3, lines 97–98)	**Irony:**

FOLLOW-UP: How does Shakespeare's use of dramatic irony help you understand the characters and plot of the play?

Literary Elements Worksheet 4

The Tragedy of Hamlet

Imagery

Imagery is the use of language that often appeals to the senses, to evoke a picture or concrete sensation of a person, thing, place, or experience.

Record and explain passages that contain imagery of each of the five senses. The first one has been done for you.

SIGHT

Example: *"Mad as the sea and wind when both contend / Which is the mightier." (Act IV, Scene 1, lines 7–8)*	**Image created:** *Gertrude is describing Hamlet's madness by creating the image of crashing waves and howling wind. The audience can visualize the waves being churned up by the wind.*

HEARING

Example:	Image created:

TOUCH

Example:	Image created:

TASTE

Example:	Image created:

SMELL

Example:	Image created:

FOLLOW-UP: Which of the play's themes is reflected in the sensory images you recorded above? How do these images contribute to the mood of the play?

Literary Elements Worksheet 5

The Tragedy of Hamlet

Plot

In many tragedies, Shakespeare's included, the plot reaches its dramatic climax (or crisis) and resolution (or final outcome) in the fifth act of the play.

Identify and describe the components of the play's conclusion found in Act V.

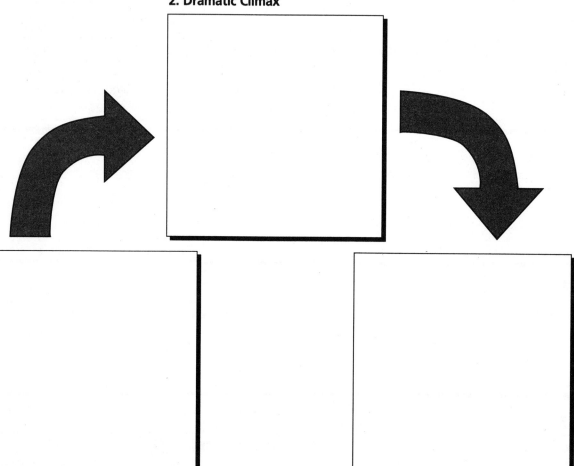

2. Dramatic Climax

1. Events Leading up to Dramatic Climax

3. Resolution

FOLLOW-UP: How does Hamlet's behavior in this climactic fifth act compare to his behavior in the previous acts? Provide examples to support your response.

_____

_____

_____

_____

_____

Play Projects

Writing About the Play

FICTIONAL NARRATIVE

Once Upon a Time . . .

Create a fictional account that illustrates life at Elsinore some six months before the play opens. Focus your attention on Old Hamlet, Claudius, Gertrude, Hamlet, and Ophelia. Use hints in the play about the personality traits and interrelationships of these characters to write your fictional account.
(Creative Writing)

LITERARY ANALYSIS

Cut! Cut!

Imagine that you are the director of a production of *Hamlet.* On the first run-through, the play runs over three hours in length and you decide that this is too long. You want the play to run for two and one-half hours and you have to cut some scenes accordingly. Which scenes would you cut? What, if anything would you be sacrificing? How would you compensate for whatever is lost? Explain your plans and reasons in a brief essay.
(Creative/Critical Writing)

SUMMARIZE

Behind the Scenes

Ophelia and Horatio are offstage for considerable periods of time. Consider the dramatic reasons for their absences. Then write a summary of their respective actions during the time we don't see them. Discuss what changes, if any, are taking place for each character.
(Creative Writing)

LITERARY ANALYSIS

Denmark Redeemed

In the course of a provocative essay on *Hamlet* in his book *The Idea of a Theater,* the critic Francis Fergusson touches on a religious element in the play. According to Fergusson, Hamlet sees the evil—the rottenness of life—in the state of Denmark, bears witness, suffers to reveal the truth as a kind of agent in the hands of a higher spiritual power, and becomes a martyr to this cause as the natural order and spiritual health are restored. In an essay, discuss how much evidence you can find for the development of this pattern in the play.
(Critical Writing)

COMPARE/CONTRAST

Shakespeare Then and Now

Read a contemporary play that shows the influence of Shakespeare's *Hamlet,* such as *Winterset,* by Maxwell Anderson; *Henry IV,* by Luigi Pirandello; or *Rosencrantz & Guildenstern Are Dead,* by Tom Stoppard. Compare the work of your choice with Shakespeare's play.
(Critical Writing)

COMPARE/CONTRAST

Comparing Characters

In an essay compare the following characters: Claudius and Macbeth as men driven by ambition; Hamlet and Macbeth as sensitive men who, at times, because of the terrible circumstances in which they find themselves, appear to lose touch with reality; and Ophelia and Lady Macbeth, who both break down into insanity. In your essay, be sure to discuss why you think that Ophelia and Lady Macbeth collapse while Hamlet and Macbeth, who also reveal symptoms of breakdown and madness, nonetheless persist.
(Critical Writing)

Cross-Curricular Connections

GEOGRAPHY

Where in the World?

Find a political map that accurately portrays western Europe around 1600. Locate Denmark, Wittenberg, Elsinore (sometimes shown as Helsingør), Norway, Poland, France, and England. Then find the most reasonable routes for each of the following journeys: Hamlet's journey from Wittenberg to Elsinore; Laertes' journey from France to Elsinore; Fortinbras's journey through Denmark and on to Poland; Rosencrantz and Guildenstern's journey from Elsinore to England.

SCIENCE AND HISTORY

Conflicting Cosmologies

In a paper entitled "Hamlet and Infinite Universe," Peter D. Usher, professor of astronomy and astrophysics at Pennsylvania State University, offers his interpretation of *Hamlet*. Usher suggests that *Hamlet* is an allegory for the competition between the cosmological models of Copernicus and Ptolemy. He points out that Wittenberg, where Hamlet studied, was a center for Copernican learning. Claudius, Usher suggests, was named for Claudius Ptolemy, who perfected the geocentric model.
Use reference sources or science textbooks to gather information about the world views of Copernicus and Ptolemy. As you compare the two, consider how these ideas might relate to *Hamlet*.

HUMANITIES

Classical Allusions

An allusion is a reference to a statement, a person, a place, an event, or a thing that is known from literature, history, religion, myth, sports, science, or popular culture. Shakespeare uses allusions to provide parallels to characters or events in his plays. Read the following italicized allusions from *Hamlet,* and then use reference books to help you understand them. Write an explanation of each allusion.

> 'Twas *Aeneas'* tale to *Dido,* and thereabout of it especially where he speaks of *Priam's* slaughter.
> (Act II, Scene 2, lines 458–460)

> What's *Hecuba* to him, or he to *Hecuba*
> That he should weep for her?
> (Act II, Scene 2, lines 573–574)

> I would have such a fellow whipped for o'erdoing *Termagant.* It out-herods *Herod.*
> (Act III, Scene 2, lines 14–15)

> And my imaginations are as foul
> As *Vulcan's* smithy.
> (Act III, Scene 2, lines 88–89)

ART

The Clothes Make the Character

Create costume designs for each character in *Hamlet,* changing the look of the costumes as necessary from scene to scene. First, decide whether you will design costumes for a traditional presentation of the play or show the characters set in a different period of time. Then, for each scene, sketch the characters in the appropriate setting, giving a general idea of what the costumes look like. Next, provide detailed individual drawings for each character's costume.

MUSIC

Hamlet and *Hair*

Locate a recording of the rock opera *Hair.* Listen to the selection "What a Piece of Work Is Man," and then locate the section of text in *Hamlet* from which the lyrics are taken. With a group, discuss how your interpretation of the lines is changed, if at all, by listening to the music. If you are familiar with the story of the rock opera, compare the meaning of the lyrics in *Hair* with the lines in *Hamlet.*

Multimedia and Internet Connections

NOTE: Check with your teacher about school policies on accessing Internet sites.

FILM: REVIEW

To See, or Not to See

Watch one of the film adaptations of *Hamlet.* Recent versions, such as those in which Kenneth Branagh or Mel Gibson star as Hamlet, should be available at your local library or at movie-rental stores. Compare the movie to the written play. Do you find one form easier to understand and appreciate than the other? Explain. How do the characters and settings differ from what you imagined as you were reading the play? What parts of the movie, if any, would you like to see presented in another way? If you were reviewing the movie, would you recommend that others see it? Why or why not?

SEARCH: INTERNET

Elsinore, Yesterday and Today

Elsinore, the setting of *Hamlet,* has existed as a major presence in shipping and travel industries for centuries. Using the Internet, locate information about Elsinore's present role as an important shipping port and about Elsinore's history, architecture, and culture. Select one aspect of Elsinore, past or present, that appeals to you. Save related articles and images that you find to a file on your computer. Then create a digital report by arranging the text and image files in an interesting, accessible, and informative fashion. As you do your search, be sure to include *Denmark* as one of your key words as cities named Elsinore exist in various parts of the world. You probably will want to restrict your search to articles written in English.

PERFORMANCE: VIDEO

Elsinore Week in Review

If the happenings in the castle at Elsinore occurred today, imagine how the Sunday news/talk shows would cover the events. With a group of your classmates, create and videotape a news-related talk show focusing on the death of Claudius and the emergence of Fortinbras as the new king of Denmark. One person in your group will be the moderator; others will be news reporters or correspondents with a variety of political positions. Once you have developed and rehearsed the contents of the program, you can begin to tape. One or more technicians will be responsible for capturing the production on videotape, for creating the opening and closing credits, and for selecting and including the program's theme music. Show the final, edited version of your program to the class.

RESEARCH: INTERNET

Extend *Hamlet* with Hyperlinks

Several sites devoted to *Hamlet* provide a wealth of information related to the play. Some sites are designed specifically for students, and these offer information that you might find particularly interesting. Others are designed for research and allow you to search the text of the plays and use hyperlinks to jump to glossaries. Many include interactive pages where you can ask or answer questions. Create an index of sites for others to use while studying *Hamlet.* Give the title of each site, the Internet address, and a short description of the sites' contents.

Introducing the Connections

The **Connections** at the end of the HRW Library edition of this book create the opportunity for students to relate its themes to other genres, times, and places and to their own lives. The following chart will facilitate your use of these additional works. Succeeding pages offer **Making Meanings** questions to stimulate student response.

Selection	Summary, Connection to Play
Just Lather, That's All Hernando Téllez *short story*	Telléz is famous for putting ordinary people in horrific situations, and this story of a barber confronting an oppressor demonstrates this technique. The main character suffers a dilemma similar to Hamlet's; he must decide if patriotism justifies murder.
Plays and Performances John Russell Brown *book excerpt*	A colorful account of the theater in Shakespeare's time that banishes notions that Shakespeare produced incomprehensible plays for the elite. Brown's account of the circumstances of the early modern English theater allows us to see Shakespeare's plays with clearer, if less reverent, eyes.
In a Dark Time Theodore Roethke *poem*	Roethke's haunting poem contemplates the trails of madness and leads to the heart of some of the identity crises in *Hamlet*.
Raymond Chandler's *Hamlet* Jonathan Vos Post *short story*	This parodic short story blends Chandler's hard-boiled style with Shakespeare's plot. It tells the story in a mock-serious tone and employs an abundance of detective-fiction clichés.
from **John Gielgud Directs Richard Burton in** *Hamlet:* **A Journal of Rehearsals** Richard L. Sterne *book excerpt*	Understanding how and why a director makes decisions about the script, costuming, and setting can help us focus on aspects of the play we may not have seen as open for interpretation. Gielgud's clear account of his own production concept helps bridge the gap between reading and seeing.
Two Poems by Maya Angelou *poems*	Angelou unveils minds tormented and made eloquent by sleeplessness and grief in these paired poems—"Insomniac" and "Mourning Grace." The struggle to find one's own place amid turbulent emotions resonates deeply with Shakespeare's often tumultuous play.

Introducing the Connections (cont.)

Selection	Summary, Connection to Play
The Olivier *Hamlet* Bosley Crowther *movie review*	This account of Olivier's production reminds us that the now common occurrence of filming Shakespeare's plays was originally an odd and risky undertaking. Crowther conveys both the excitement of seeing Shakespeare on screen and the details of Olivier's influential interpretation.
Fear No More the Heat o' the Sun William Shakespeare *excerpt from play*	One of the most beloved songs from Shakespeare's plays, this elegiac lyric from *Cymbeline* uses the pains of life as a way to find comfort in a loved one's death. It both echoes and contradicts the sentiments in Hamlet's most famous soliloquy.
The Gibson *Hamlet* Roger Ebert *movie review*	Ebert's vivid account of Gibson's popular production demonstrates how a less cerebral, more ordinary Prince of Denmark can add dimension to our understanding of the play.
The Branagh *Hamlet* Roger Ebert *movie review*	Branagh's movie was famous for containing the entire play, and Ebert suggests some of the practical payoffs to viewing the complete and polished version.
Sonnet 146 William Shakespeare *poem*	Shakespeare suggests that death can be defeated by teaching the body to serve the soul. Many of this poem's oppositions and resolutions are explored at greater length in *Hamlet*.

Making Meanings

1. Do you think it was right for the barber to let Captain Torres go?

2. The barber is struggling with two distinct images he has of himself. What are they?

3. Why do you think that the details of the conflict are not revealed?

READING CHECK

a. Why does Captain Torres come into the shop?

b. Why is Captain Torres's beard so thick?

c. Why does the barber keep his status as a rebel quiet?

d. What has Captain Torres done to the rebels he has caught?

Plays and Performances

1. Explain why you think going to the theater in Shakespeare's time would or would not be an enjoyable experience for you.

2. How do you think the manner of rehearsal would affect the performances?

3. How might seeing *Hamlet* on an Elizabethan stage shape the audience's interpretations and emotional reactions to the play?

READING CHECK

a. Who typically went to the theater in Shakespeare's time?

b. Why was a performance of *Richard the Second* banned from the stage?

c. Why did clergymen discourage people from attending the theater?

d. How did the companies announce that they were ready to perform?

Making Meanings

Connecting with the Play

The poet suggests that madness may be "nobility of soul / At odds with circum-stance." How does this compare with Hamlet's question about "whether it is nobler in the mind" to live and suffer or to end his life?

1. In as much detail as you can, describe the scene that the poem depicts and explain how it makes you feel.

2. A **metaphor** is a figure of speech that makes a comparison between two unlike things without the use of such specific words of comparison as *like, as, than,* or *resembles.* This poem uses an extended metaphor (called a conceit) to talk about someone searching for something. What does the speaker say he is searching for, and what does it stand for?

3. The poet comes to a "place among the rocks"* and wonders if he sees "a cave, / Or a winding path?"* What is the significance of these contrasting images?

4. Briefly discuss whether the poet's dilemma is solved at the end of the poem.

READING CHECK

a. Who or what does the poet meet "in a dark time"?*

b. What happens "in broad day"?*

c. What emotion does the poet say he feels with "purity"?*

Raymond Chandler's Hamlet

Connecting with the Play

Write a similarly brief account of the play from Ophelia's or Gertrude's point of view.

1. Briefly describe what you do and do not like about this story.

2. Why does the narrator say Hamlet's father died "with an earful of murder"?

3. **Tone** is a literary term that describes the attitude the writer takes towards the reader, subject, or character. What is the tone of this story?

READING CHECK

a. Who narrates this short story?

b. How does the narrator describe Ophelia's relationship to Hamlet?

c. How does the narrator describe Claudius's reaction to the play within the play?

d. What does the narrator leave Horatio pondering?

Making Meanings

from *John Gielgud Directs Richard Burton in* Hamlet: *A Journal of Rehearsals*

Connecting with the Play

Imagine that you are a member of the cast for Gielgud's production. Give a brief sketch of the character you will portray, and describe how you will dress and behave to make your interpretation apparent to the audience.

1. Explain why you think traditional costumes are or are not important for a production of *Hamlet*.

2. What aspects of Gielgud's account of his production concept support the reviewer's description of it as "streamlined"?

3. Which of the excerpted reviews provides the best evidence to support the respective writer's interpretation of the performance?

4. Write a brief essay in which you defend or dispute Gielgud's claim that minimal scenery and props would improve the audience's understanding of *Hamlet*.

READING CHECK

a. Why does Gielgud propose acting the play with minimal costumes, lighting, and scenery?

b. Who plays Hamlet in this production?

c. Who plays the ghost?

Two Poems by Maya Angelou

Connecting with the Play

Which character from *Hamlet* would most likely identify with the sentiments in "Mourning Grace"? Explain your choice.

1. Identify some of the emotions these poems arouse, and briefly explain why you prefer one.

2. Personification means giving human feelings, thought, or attitudes to an object, animal, or an abstract idea. What abstraction is personified in "Insomniac," and what traits is it given?

3. Neither of Angelou's poems uses traditional stanzas. In what ways does the presentation of her poems complement their meanings?

READING CHECK

a. In "Insomniac," to what does Angelou compare her efforts to sleep?

b. Does the insomniac manage to sleep?

c. In "Mourning Grace," why would the speaker's tongue be salty?

d. With what question does "Mourning Grace" end?

Exploring the Connections (cont.)

The Olivier Hamlet

Making Meanings

Connecting with the Play

Would you prefer to see a Shakespeare play on film or on the stage? Explain your choice.

1. Crowther reports that in Olivier's production, his mother's treachery dismays Hamlet more than his father's death. What textual evidence supports this interpretation?

2. Crowther refers to Rosencrantz and Guildenstern as "windbags" and suggests that they are not necessary characters. Write a brief essay in which you support or challenge his view.

3. Crowther approves of Olivier's presentation of Hamlet as "a solid virile young man." Do you agree that this is an important aspect of Hamlet's character?

READING CHECK

a. Crowther suggests that Shakespeare's plays "have been more often heard than seen." What does he mean?

b. Who plays Hamlet in this production?

c. In what way was Olivier's *Hamlet* different from any previous production of the play?

d. How does Crowther think Olivier's extensive editing of Shakespeare's play affects the final production? Does it make the play harder or easier to understand?

Fear No More the Heat o' the Sun

Connecting with the Play

Set the words to music, either a melody that you compose or one that you already know.

1. Briefly discuss which of the song's images or themes you find most striking.

2. At the end of the first stanza, Guiderius compares "Golden lads and girls" and "chimney sweepers." Why do you think he makes that particular comparison?

3. This song shares with Hamlet's "To be, or not to be" soliloquy the suggestion that death can be a comfort. Compare the development of this idea in each passage, and account for Hamlet's different conclusion.

READING CHECK

a. In what play does this song appear?

b. Why are Guiderius and Arviragus singing the song?

c. Why do Guiderius and Aviragus think Fidele need no longer fear the heat of the sun?

Copyright © by Holt, Rinehart and Winston. All rights reserved.

Making Meanings

Connecting with the Play

Write a short essay on how Gibson's status as a star and actor affects your concept of the character of Hamlet.

1. Ebert says that Gibson's Hamlet is not melancholy. Briefly explain why you prefer an "upbeat" or a melancholy Hamlet.

2. How might the "substantial" physical world in this production complement the interpretation of Hamlet's character that Ebert describes?

3. Ebert says that this production makes it clear that Gertrude's attraction to Claudius is "at least as sexual as it is political." In what way might the attraction be political?

4. Ophelia's later scenes, we are told, "are with herself." What interpretation of Ophelia does this staging encourage?

READING CHECK

a. Ebert begins his review by mentioning a play other than *Hamlet*. What play does he mention?

b. Ebert mentions a scene created by the director. What scene is this?

c. What does Ebert think of the actresses who play Gertrude and Ophelia?

d. On the whole, does Ebert approve of this movie?

The Branagh Hamlet

Connecting with the Play

As a director, select a cast for your production of Hamlet from the actors named in this and previous reviews. Support your choices with excerpts from the text.

1. Ebert describes Claudius in this production as "more balanced and powerful" than he is usually presented. Explain why you prefer a Claudius that is simply evil or one that is more complicated.

2. Compare Branagh's and Gibson's emphasis on "substantial physicality" with the minimalism of Olivier's and Gielgud's productions.

3. Ebert says that Polonius is "not so much a foolish old man as an advisor out of his depth." What are some of the interpretive consequences of reading Polonius as foolish or as wise?

READING CHECK

a. According to Ebert, what is the result of positioning Hamlet in the foreground of the first scene?

b. In what way was Branagh's production "a first"?

c. In what time period is this production set?

d. What does Ebert think noteworthy about this production's play within a play?

4. Ebert claims that each of the many productions he has seen of *Hamlet* has taught him something about the play. This would suggest that many competing interpretations of the play might be more helpful than a single one that answers all interpretive questions. Write a brief essay in which you defend or dispute this suggestion.

Exploring the Connections *(cont.)*

Sonnet 146

Making Meanings

Connecting with the Play

Write your own soliloquy on the subject of living a full life.

1. What picture does this poem create for you?

2. A **metaphor** is a figure of speech that makes a comparison between two unlike things without the use of such specific words of comparison as *like, as, than,* or *resembles.* This poem develops two central metaphors, one involving a mansion with a short lease, and another involving a servant and master. In each case, what does the figure represent?

READING CHECK

a. Who or what does the sonnet proclaim as "the center of my sinful earth"?

b. What is the general idea of the questions the sonnet asks?

c. Who or what might "Eat up thy charge"?

3. The first part of this sonnet develops the idea that one should not richly furnish the body at the soul's expense. What idea does the second part of the sonnet develop?

4. Hamlet's initial attitude toward death is expressed in his "To be, or not to be" soliloquy, where he is afraid to die. Act V, Scene 2, he says, "the readiness is all" (line 228). Does the attitude about death in this sonnet resemble his attitude at the beginning or the end of the play? Explain.

Name _____ Date _____

TEST PART I: OBJECTIVE QUESTIONS

In the space provided, mark each true statement _T_ and each false statement _F. (10 points)_

_____ **1.** With the death of Old Hamlet, the next in line for the throne would be Polonius.

_____ **2.** Ophelia is torn between her feelings for Hamlet and her duty to her father.

_____ **3.** Claudius and Polonius have in common that each does not trust his own son (or stepson).

_____ **4.** Rosencrantz is one of the few trustworthy people in _Hamlet_.

_____ **5.** At the end of the play, it is clear that Fortinbras will become the new king of Denmark.

Circle the letter of the answer that best completes the statement. _(20 points)_

6. Hamlet, Laertes, and Fortinbras have in common the fact that
   a. they all go to the same college
   b. they are all patriotic Danes
   c. their fathers have all been killed
   d. their mothers have all been unfaithful

7. Laertes is best described as
   a. direct, impulsive
   b. thoughtful, melancholy
   c. wise, compassionate
   d. ambitious, cruel

8. The play-within-a-play is a device
   a. to break up the tragic action of the play
   b. to allow the main characters a break
   c. to provide comic relief
   d. to help Hamlet identify his father's murderer

9. Regarding the play-within-a-play, Claudius
   a. enjoys the show the actors put on
   b. pays no attention to the plot
   c. reveals his guilt by his actions
   d. suspects Hamlet changed the script

10. The soliloquy "To be, or not to be" is a meditation on
   a. war and peace
   b. life and death
   c. good and evil
   d. corruption and an ideal society

11. When Hamlet says "Frailty, thy name is woman" he is referring to
   a. Ophelia
   b. Osric
   c. Gertrude
   d. the Player Queen

12. Hamlet tells Ophelia, "Get thee to a nunnery" because
   a. she'd be richer there
   b. he, himself, is very religious
   c. he fears for her life
   d. she must not be a "breeder of sinners"

13. In his mother's chamber, Hamlet strikes through a screen and thinks he has killed
   a. Claudius
   b. Polonius
   c. Fortinbras
   d. Laertes

14. The Ghost reappears in Gertrude's chamber to
   a. see how his former wife is getting along
   b. whet Hamlet's "almost blunted purpose"
   c. make Hamlet's task easier
   d. sympathize with the new ghost of Polonius

15. Fortinbras's importance for Hamlet lies in the fact that
   a. Hamlet sees him as an enemy
   b. Hamlet sees him as a possible ally
   c. Hamlet learns from his decisiveness
   d. Hamlet would like to go to Poland

Name _____ Date _____

TEST PART II: SHORT-ANSWER QUESTIONS

Answer each question, using the lines provided. *(40 points)*

16. Describe the opening mood of the play and tell what helps to establish this mood.

_____

_____

_____

17. Before Hamlet hears anything from the Ghost, what are his feelings about the world in general and Denmark in particular?

_____

_____

_____

18. After Hamlet meets the players, what does he ask them to do? What does he hope to accomplish by this action?

_____

_____

_____

19. What is your opinion of Polonius? What details cause you to arrive at this opinion?

_____

_____

_____

20. How does Claudius react to the play-within-a-play? What does Hamlet surmise from Claudius's reaction?

_____

_____

_____

Name _____ Date _____

21. Why doesn't Hamlet kill Claudius when he finds Claudius at prayer?

_____

_____

_____

22. Why is Hamlet's murder of Polonius advantageous to Claudius?

_____

_____

_____

23. What behaviors indicate Ophelia's madness?

_____

_____

_____

24. On his return from France, what threat does Laertes pose to Claudius's reign as king?

_____

_____

_____

25. In what ways is Denmark's "illness" cured in the final scene?

_____

_____

_____

TEST PART III: ESSAY QUESTIONS

Choose two of the following topics. Use your own paper to write two or three paragraphs about each topic you choose. *(30 points)*

a. Discuss Shakespeare's use of humor in the gravedigger's scene as (a) a reflection of or a comment on the major themes of the play, and (b) an illustration of dramatic irony.

b. Analyze Hamlet's development—the changes in his nature—using these three soliloquies: "O that this too solid flesh would melt, . . ." (Act I, Scene 2); "O, what a rogue . . ." (Act II, Scene 2); and "How all occasions do inform against me . . ." (Act IV, Scene 4). Define the evolution of his emotional state from solitary despondency through his subsequent encounters with the visiting players and then with the forces of Fortinbras.

c. Describe, with reference to the text, Hamlet's relationships with women.

d. Compare the disintegration of Ophelia in Act IV, Scene 5, and that of Lady Macbeth in the sleep-walking scene in *Macbeth* (Act V, Scene 1), discussing how their ravings reflect the causes of their breakdowns.

e. Examine the ways in which the secondary characters Polonius, Rosencrantz and Guildenstern, Horatio, and Fortinbras are used by Shakespeare to reflect the concerns of the main plot and themes of the play, as well as Hamlet's own development.

f. Discuss how one of the **Connections** (HRW LIBRARY edition) is related to a theme, issue, or character in *The Tragedy of Hamlet*.

Use this space to make notes.

Answer Key

Answer Key

The Tragedy of Hamlet

Act I

■ Making Meanings

READING CHECK

a. Old Hamlet defeated King Fortinbras of Norway in battle and won the rights to certain lands for Denmark. Now Fortinbras's son is preparing to attack Denmark to avenge his father's death and to recapture the lost territory.

b. Old Hamlet had no chance to confess his sins and be pardoned prior to dying.

c. Claudius first addresses the delicate matter of his marriage to Gertrude, his brother's widow, less than two months after the death of Old Hamlet. Claudius then turns to the issue of young Fortinbras's military threat to the kingdom. He announces that he is sending ambassadors to the sickly king of Norway, Fortinbras's uncle, with a message asking the king to restrain his nephew.

d. Claudius would rather have Hamlet stay at Elsinore than return to Wittenberg. His professed reason is that Hamlet should enjoy the privileges of being the heir apparent to the throne. His underlying reason, however, may be that he wants to keep an eye on Hamlet.

e. Polonius tells Ophelia to be wary of Hamlet. He warns his daughter that she should not trust the prince's professions of love because Hamlet's status as the heir apparent casts doubt on his sincerity as a suitor. He forbids Ophelia to speak with Hamlet for the time being or to receive messages from him.

f. While Old Hamlet slept in his garden, he was murdered by his treacherous brother Claudius, who poured a deadly poison called hebona into his ear. The official account of his death is that he was bitten by a poisonous serpent.

g. The father sets the task of avenging his death.

---

1. Responses will vary. Some students may cite Hamlet's references to suicide, his melancholy behavior, and his unexplained plan to feign madness as indicators of insanity. Others may suggest that Hamlet is pretending to be mad so that he

can express the violent emotions he would otherwise be forced to contain.

2. Scene 1 sets a dark, troubled, and mysterious mood. It also provides the political background of the plot.

3. Hamlet is characterized initially as quick witted. He is adept at puns, double meanings, and irony. In his first soliloquy, he reveals his true feelings of anguish at his father's death and his mother's remarriage to Claudius, a union he sees as tainted and corrupt. He is so depressed that he wishes he could commit suicide. The soliloquy portrays Hamlet as deeply sensitive, melancholy, and passionate. Later, when the prince learns of the ghostly figure resembling Old Hamlet seen on the battlements, he becomes feverishly excited. Through following speeches, Hamlet is characterized as capable of decisive and courageous action, although cautious not to give away information or to show his true feelings. He hints that he has no respect for Claudius but does defer to Gertrude when she asks him to stay in Denmark.

4. In seeking a peaceful solution to Fortinbras's aggression, Claudius reveals himself to be politic in state matters and concerned enough with public opinion to get his council's approval of his marriage to Gertrude; he is adept at flattery with Laertes and Polonius and is wary enough of Hamlet to want him close at hand. He finds any excuse for drink—even Hamlet's insolence.

5. Putting on an "antic disposition" means that Hamlet will feign madness. By convincing Claudius and others at the court that he is not to be taken seriously, Hamlet hopes to find out more about the true circumstances of his father's death. Such a quest would be dangerous, if not impossible, were he considered sane.

6. Students may identify examples such as the following: "'Tis an unweeded garden / That grows to seed; things rank and gross in nature / Possess

128 | The Tragedy of Hamlet

it merely." (Act I, Scene 2) "Something is rotten in the state of Denmark." (Act I, Scene 4) "leprous distillment . . . lazar-like" (Act I, Scene 5). Images of disease and decay reflect the corruption and sinful behavior of characters in the play.

7. Students may contrast Hamlet's disgust and almost suicidal despair in his first soliloquy with his renewed sense of purpose in the second, after the Ghost has solemnly charged him, "Remember me."

8. A possible answer would point out that Hamlet felt great love and respect for his father. In Scene 2 he calls him "so excellent a king" and tells Horatio, "I shall not look upon his like again." Old Hamlet's death has obviously caused him profound grief. When Hamlet learns the true circumstances of his father's death in Scene 5, he emotionally declares his readiness to take vengeance on Claudius. In this respect, his situation resembles that of young Fortinbras, who is collecting troops to try to recapture the territory his father lost to Old Hamlet. Both young men are trying to avenge what they perceive as injustices done to their fathers. Laertes is portrayed as a loving and obedient son, patiently listening to his father's long-winded advice and humbly taking his leave for France. One has the impression that Laertes is dominated, or perhaps even bullied, by Polonius.

9. Students may point out that Ophelia probably feels annoyed and embarrassed. Both her brother and her father speak to her as if she is in imminent danger of losing her virginity to Hamlet. Neither man evinces any trust for Ophelia's judgment. Ophelia's protest that Hamlet's attentions have seemed entirely honorable so far falls on deaf ears. Notice, however, that Ophelia is not portrayed as utterly submissive. After Laertes' warnings, for example, she calmly urges him to follow his own advice by behaving modestly, lest he prove hypocritical (Scene 3). Students will

probably agree that many young women today face problems from overprotective or suspicious parents or siblings, particularly in cultures that still regard young women as under the control of their nearest male relatives.

10. Many students, having heard the action of the play described in terms of delay, cowardice, or intellectual rationalization, may be tempted to characterize Hamlet's approach to his problems in such terms. You may want to point out that Hamlet is portrayed as many-sided in the first act: He is witty, melancholy, and intellectual but also courageous and decisive when he meets the Ghost. Students may suggest that Hamlet's predicament at the warlike, almost primitive court of Elsinore would be quite different from such a problem in a contemporary setting. In the world of the play, all authority stems from the king; the knowledge that the king is corrupt inevitably confronts Hamlet with great danger, and he must resort to unusual means to survive and take revenge.

■ Reading Strategies Worksheets

Making Inferences

Claudius: Through his speeches in scene 2, Claudius appears cautious, shrewd, practical, and hypocritical. Claudius attempts to talk Hamlet out of his grief, saying that Hamlet is being stubborn and arrogant by continuing to mourn for his father. Hamlet describes Claudius's debauched revels, and the Ghost recounts Claudius's murderous actions. Students might infer that Claudius is self-interested, corrupt, and untrustworthy.

Gertrude: The queen quickly remarries and appears to have forgotten her late husband and religious ideals, prompting Hamlet to describe her as fickle and immoral. He is personally outraged that she has married Claudius. Students might infer that she is self-absorbed and motivated by a desire for physical comforts.

Answer Key (cont.)

Polonius: Through his speech to Laertes, which is full of clichés and banal moralizing, Polonius is characterized as pompous and rather foolish. He callously tries to convince Ophelia that Hamlet is merely leading her on, and he orders her to break off all contact with the young prince. He appears suspicious, meddlesome, and insensitive, and he is worried that Ophelia's relationship with Hamlet will embarrass him. Students might infer that he has an inflated opinion of himself. They might also infer that he would do anything to please those in power.

Laertes: Laertes is portrayed as an affectionate, if overprotective, brother in his speech to Ophelia. His deference to his father shows that he is a respectful son. Students might infer that he has a touch of Polonius's pomposity (which he reveals in his conversation with his sister) but is basically an intelligent and good-hearted young man.

Ophelia: Although Ophelia appears to be a rather flat character, she does show that she is capable of lightly ironic humor when she teases Laertes about his moralizing advice. Laertes warns her not to be gullible when it comes to Hamlet's declarations of love, and she meekly accepts his admonitions. Students might infer that she is submissive, one-dimensional, and easily manipulated.

FOLLOW-UP: These characters, who make up the Danish ruling family and part of the court, exhibit such a variety of weaknesses that it seems unlikely the country is being governed effectively. Both the king and queen appear self-involved and more concerned with their personal problems than with the government of the country. Hamlet seems too melancholy and preoccupied to be an effective ruler. Polonius makes a pompous, shallow, and inept advisor.

■ Test: Act I

A. *(20 points)*

1. c
2. b
3. a
4. b
5. d

B. *(50 points)*

6. The mood is dark and ominous.

7. The midnight setting and the talk of warfare and the supernatural help to establish the mood.

8. Claudius has sent a letter to the bedridden king of Norway, asking the king to restrain his nephew, Fortinbras, who is demanding the return of lands won from Norway by Old Hamlet.

9. Hamlet is despairing and weary of the world. He is particularly distressed over his mother's hasty remarriage to Claudius. He condemns his mother and Claudius for their moral weakness.

10. Laertes and Hamlet are sons of members of the court. They have both returned to Elsinore after having been away to study—Hamlet in Germany and Laertes in France.

11. Ophelia's dilemma is that she is attracted to Hamlet, but a relationship cannot develop because he is royalty and she is not. She decides to obey her father and break off contact with Hamlet.

12. The Ghost identifies himself as Old Hamlet's spirit.

13. The Ghost charges Hamlet to avenge his death.

14. The Ghost admonishes Hamlet not to harm his mother, Gertrude.

15. The overall purpose of Act I is to introduce the characters and establish the conflict, the problem to be solved.

C. *(30 points)*

Answers to these questions will vary. Individual answers should indicate the student's understanding of the events in Act I and the character's personalities and motivations. The best answers will be supported by examples or lines from the play.

a. Answers should indicate students' awareness that Hamlet is not so much an action-adventure story as a psychological drama. The gripping Ghost scene sets up the conflict and leads to the rising action of the play. The action of the play would probably be much less suspenseful if the audience had already witnessed the murder scene. After all, at this point the audience is not *absolutely* sure that the Ghost is telling the truth.

b. Answers should include mention of the fact that the Ghost is silent in Scene 1, which adds a note of mystery to the feelings voiced by the watchers on the platform and effectively foreshadows the events in Scenes 4 and 5 when the mysteries are revealed.

c. Answers should indicate an awareness of most or all of the following: Hamlet is experiencing a profound grief (indicated through his dialogue with Gertrude). The soliloquy that follow illustrates his suicidal depression. Hamlet's extreme sadness is effectively paralyzing so that he does not act decisively. He is shown to be devoted to his true friends, as evidenced by his interactions with Marcellus, Bernardo, and Horatio. He felt deep love and loyalty to his deceased father. He has a great capacity for outrage which may lead to action.

d. Answers should indicate students' awareness that Hamlet's issues have little to do with the state and everything to do with family: his father's murder and his mother incestuous remarriage to the murderer. In the dialogues and soliloquies woven into the play, the audience is continually made aware of Hamlet's obsession with his private issues. He appears to have no interest in the throne for the sake of power and authority.

Act II

■ Making Meanings

> **READING CHECK**
>
> **a.** Reynaldo is one of Polonius's servants. His job is to travel to Paris to spy on Laertes and then to report to Polonius on the young man's behavior.
>
> **b.** Ophelia reports that Hamlet appeared unexpectedly at the door of her private chamber while she was sewing. Hamlet's jacket was entirely unlaced, he wore no hat, his stockings were in disarray, he was pale, and his knees were knocking. He took Ophelia by the wrist, held her hard, sighed pitifully, and then left her without a word.
>
> **c.** Just as Polonius wants Reynaldo to spy on Laertes, so Claudius wants Rosencrantz and Guildenstern to spy on Hamlet.
>
> **d.** Polonius tells Claudius and Gertrude that he will arrange an encounter between Hamlet and Ophelia. Polonius himself will then hide behind a curtain during the meeting to eavesdrop on their conversation and find out more about Hamlet's state of mind.
>
> **e.** According to Polonius, Hamlet's "transformation" is due to lovesickness for Ophelia.
>
> **f.** Hamlet proposes to test Claudius's guilt by having the players perform a drama, the plot of which contains similarities to the murder of Old Hamlet. Hamlet will watch Claudius's behavior closely as the king witnesses the play.

1. Responses will vary. Some students may be negatively impressed by Polonius, who is revealed through his actions as shallow and meddlesome. Others may be positively impressed by Hamlet, whose intelligence is apparent in his quick-witted remarks, intuitive reactions, and clever plans.

2. Responses will vary. Among the instances of Hamlet's humor that students may cite are the following: (a) his statement that Rosencrantz and Guildenstern live in the "secret parts of Fortune"; the joke is that, since the courtiers have "middling fortune" (neither especially good nor bad), they are linked with the middle part of the body of

Fortune, personified here as a strumpet or prostitute; (b) the play on the idea that a beggar, lacking ambition which is but a shadow, is more real than a monarch or a hero—figures who are composed entirely of ambition and amount to shadows.

3. Through his actions toward his children and Hamlet and through his speeches in the court, Polonius is revealed to be controlling, arrogant, pompous, smug, and artificial—a caricature of a wise and confident lord chamberlain.

4. When Hamlet visits Ophelia, his "madness" is evident by his silence and his pale, disheveled, and mournful appearance. Others attribute this behavior to Hamlet's unrequited love for Ophelia. In the lobby, Hamlet plays the lunatic clown in his meeting with Polonius. When he meets with Rosencrantz and Guildenstern, Hamlet again seems melancholy but says he does not know the reason for his misery. Hamlet might be using these appearances of madness to show his contempt for those around him, or perhaps he is unable to control his runaway emotions—or perhaps the truth lies somewhere in between.

5. Responses will vary. A possible answer would be that Hamlet has subordinated his love for Ophelia to the strategic necessity of convincing Claudius and the court that he is mad. In addition, his mother's remarriage, which he regards as loathsome, may have turned him against thoughts of romance or marriage for himself. He may also distrust Ophelia because he fears that she will report any secrets he confides in her to her father.

6. Possible answers include the following: Rosencrantz and Guildenstern, with whom Hamlet has been friends since early youth, have been revealed as spies of the king; the troupe of players has been banned from the city, and they could not act there in any case since their places had been taken by child performers; people who once scorned Claudius now pay a fortune for

small pictures of him. The root cause of the disorder, of course, is the reign of Claudius himself.

7. Claudius is using Rosencrantz and Guildenstern to find out more about Hamlet's true mental state. Polonius is using Reynaldo to spy on Laertes' behavior in France, and he is using Ophelia to provoke Hamlet into revealing the cause of his madness. In his soliloquy at the end of Scene 2, Hamlet announces to the audience his intention to use the players to find out the truth about Claudius's involvement in the murder of Old Hamlet.

8. In general, each of the "fishing" parties involves characters acting, playing a part, or putting on a mask. For example, Claudius pretends friendship for Rosencrantz and Guildenstern, who in turn pretend friendship for Hamlet, who in turn pretends to be mad. Reynaldo will have to play a part, scripted largely by Polonius, to find out the truth about Laertes' behavior in Paris. And Hamlet himself intends to make a theatrical production the test of the truth or falsehood of Claudius's guilt. Queen Gertrude is the only major character totally removed from the make-believe; even Ophelia will be used by her father as bait for Hamlet. Claudius, Polonius, Hamlet, Reynaldo, Rosencrantz, and Guildenstern are all wearing masks of some kind or another.

9. Responses will vary. Most students will agree that young adults today would feel resentful of such intrusive behaviors as parents asking friends to spy on their children's behavior and report back. Most would feel that they had been betrayed by both their friends and their parents.

10. Responses will vary, but most will include references to the United States breaking away from British rule and, subsequently, rejecting much of the social structure surrounding the monarchy. When early Americans revolted against the British crown, they did so for a variety of reasons, includ-

ing self-rule by a democratically elected government. The idea that one could achieve rank and power based on hard work and personal achievement was strongly motivating to early colonists, and this ideal has become a part of the American cultural heritage. Young people in the United States today might find it unthinkable that society could make judgments about possibilities open to them based solely on their family's social standing.

■ Reading Strategies Worksheet

Summarizing

Claudius will spy on Hamlet.

Plan: Claudius arranges for Rosencrantz and Guildenstern to spy on Hamlet. He has also arranged with Polonius to have Ophelia delay Hamlet with conversation so that the two older men might eavesdrop on the couple's exchange.

Reason: Claudius wants to be assured of Hamlet's madness; if Hamlet is insane, Claudius wants to know whether Ophelia's rejection of Hamlet has caused the young prince's malady.

Polonius will spy on Laertes (and Hamlet).

Plan: Polonius sends Reynaldo to watch Laertes from a distance and talk to his friends in hopes of getting them to gossip about Laertes' activities in France. Polonius also conspires with Claudius to spy on Ophelia and Hamlet.

Reason: Polonius is a busybody who wants to know about his son's habits, which he assumes are debauched, and he will use his daughter in any way that might help him gain favor with the king.

FOLLOW-UP: Polonius's plan to spy on Laertes has little or no importance in terms of plot development, although it does reveal Polonius's suspicious and intrusive personality. Claudius's plans to spy on Hamlet define Claudius as Hamlet's antagonist. Hamlet's plan to expose Claudius as Old Hamlet's murderer, however, is the most important of the plans. It advances the rising action of the plot as

Hamlet becomes certain of his right to take revenge on Claudius for his father's death.

■ Test: Act II

A. (20 points)

1. c
2. a
3. b
4. c
5. b

B. (50 points)

6. Polonius is convinced that Hamlet has gone mad because of his love for Ophelia.

7. Claudius has recruited Rosencrantz and Guildenstern to spy on Hamlet and discover the cause of his transformation.

8. Polonius will have Ophelia "accidentally" encounter Hamlet in a place where Polonius and Claudius can eavesdrop on their interaction.

9. Polonius now seems shallow, foolish, and meddlesome; at the beginning of the play, he seemed to be a more reasonable and intelligent character.

10. Hamlet acts wild and crazed in Ophelia's room. He acts contemptuous and mocking toward Polonius, Rosencrantz, and Guildenstern. He speaks in cryptic and nonsensical ways.

11. Hamlet wants the players to perform a play called *The Murder of Gonzago*.

12. The play will duplicate in many details the murder of Old Hamlet by Claudius. Hamlet hopes to determine the king's guilt or innocence by watching his response to the play.

13. Gertrude thinks Hamlet's father's death and her quick marriage are the causes of his odd behavior.

14. Claudius probably fears that Hamlet knows that Claudius killed Old Hamlet.

15. The theme of life as theater, or appearance versus reality, is emphasized with the entry of the

Answer Key (cont.)

The Tragedy of Hamlet

players, the discussion about the play, and Hamlet's continued act of madness.

C. (30 points)

Answers to these questions will vary. Individual answers should indicate the student's understanding of the events in Act II and the character's personalities and motivations. The best answers will be supported by examples or lines from the play.

a. Answers should indicate that Polonius is rather harmless, if nosy and meddlesome. Claudius, on the other hand, is a crafty, completely rational criminal who is spying on Hamlet as one would spy on a natural enemy.

b. Answers should make reference to Hamlet's explanation at the end of Act II, Scene 2, in which he describes how he plans to evoke a guilty reaction from Claudius by having him watch a play that contains a reenactment of the murder. Hamlet points out that he needs this evidence because the Ghost might, in fact, be the devil. Some may find his reasoning convincing, but most will see it as just more procrastination born of Hamlet's introspective nature, his "weakness and melancholy."

c. Answers should indicate an awareness that Polonius talks in circles. He loves the sound of his own voice and delights in lofty-sounding phrases. In short, he does not get to the point.

d. Opinions should be supported with reasons and examples from the text. Most will find that Act I is more suspenseful because it opens with a mystery wrapped in a ghost story. The action of Act II is much less dramatic, although it sets the stage for a return to tension, mystery, and high drama in the following act.

Act III

■ Making Meanings

> **READING CHECK**
>
> a. Ophelia is being used as bait for Hamlet by Claudius and Polonius. The two men disregard any feelings of love that may exist between the young woman and the prince. Instead, they want her to converse with Hamlet so that they can spy on him, to determine whether or not he is really mad.
>
> b. In this soliloquy, Hamlet regards death as a deliverance from the frustrations, insults, and woes of life. On the other hand, he muses on death as frightening and dreadful: It is "The undiscovered country, from whose bourn/No traveler returns." Hamlet says that, but for his fear of the unknown after death, many people like himself would commit suicide rather than continue to endure the miseries of life.
>
> c. After he observes Hamlet with Ophelia, Claudius suspects that Hamlet may be more dangerous than lovesick. He therefore decides to send him to England to collect unpaid tribute.
>
> d. Hamlet advises the actors to follow a middle course in their speeches. They should avoid undue bombast, but at the same time they should not be too tame. They should "suit the action to the word, the word to the action"; their delivery should be appropriate to the situation. They should also stick closely to the script that is set down for them.
>
> e. Hamlet does not want to take revenge while Claudius is at his prayers because, if Claudius dies in a state of grace, his soul will go to heaven. This would deprive Hamlet and the ghost of his father of true revenge.

1. Responses will vary. Some students may note that they saw Hamlet from the beginning as a bright and interesting but melancholy character. In this act, however, Hamlet shows a cruel, almost violent streak in his interactions with Ophelia and Gertrude. This may make students think less favorably of him.

2. Hamlet admires Horatio's endurance, judgment, forthrightness, and loyalty. In comparison with Horatio, Rosencrantz and Guildenstern are disloyal and sycophantic.

3. Responses will vary. Most students will agree that the turning point, or structural climax, of the play occurs in this act when Claudius reveals his guilt by rising and leaving the players' production of *The Murder of Gonzago*. This moment is crucial to the plot because it shows Hamlet that the claims of the Ghost are true, rather than being the deceptive wiles of the devil. From this moment on, Hamlet must shoulder the responsibility of carrying out the Ghost's demand for revenge. By the same token, the production of the play reveals to Claudius his nephew's knowledge of the crime. Though he is forced to dissemble throughout much of the second half of the play, Claudius's own interests now require that he become Hamlet's deadly antagonist. The structural climax of the play, therefore, clearly outlines the central conflict of the play. The second half of the tragedy will pit Hamlet (protagonist) in a struggle to the death with Claudius (antagonist).

4. A possible answer would contrast Hamlet's oblique irony and contempt in his confrontation with Ophelia with his openly angry reproaches of his mother later in Act III. Feigning madness in his confrontation with Ophelia, Hamlet resorts to puns and double meanings. The general drift of his comments, though, is clear: He distrusts women as lustful and treacherous.

5. A possible answer is that although Hamlet reflects on suicide in general terms, never using *I* or *me*, he now realizes that he risks his own life in killing Claudius (it will very likely be a suicide mission) and "the dread of something after death" may paralyze his action.

6. Students should point out that Hamlet's first address to Ophelia seems a natural outgrowth of the soliloquy: He asks her to pray for his sins. (Hamlet may be referring to the religious belief that suicide, which he has just been contemplating in his soliloquy, is a grave sin.) As the conversation proceeds, however, Hamlet soon shows that he is pretending madness: Perhaps he is suspicious of eavesdroppers. Some students may believe that he goes too far, especially in his condemnation of female lustfulness and in his repeated suggestion that Ophelia should live out her life as a nun.

7. Responses will vary, but most students will agree that Hamlet's graphic descriptions of the sexual relations Gertrude enjoys with Claudius may appear to be overdone. Gertrude's amazement at Hamlet's accusation of Claudius suggests that she has no knowledge of the murder.

8. A possible answer is that Claudius will now have a legitimate reason to rid himself of Hamlet either by banishment or imprisonment. Gertrude, who now knows that Claudius is a murderer, will have no one to turn to. Ophelia will be heartbroken; Laertes will seek retribution. Hamlet's friends must choose sides and reveal their true colors.

9. Responses will vary. Most students will agree that people in positions of power within a modern government are generally held accountable for their behavior. Also, women are held in higher regard in modern Western society than they have been at other times in history. It is likely that rumors leaked about a young woman being used to benefit the political purposes of two high-placed officials would make front-page news and cause the officials a good deal of grief.

10. Responses will vary but should be supported with reasons. Some will say that Hamlet's melancholy disposition and excessive grief are believable and keep him from acting in a decisive and straight-forward way. Others might say that Hamlet is intellectually skeptical and shows restraint because he is unsure of the Ghost's purpose in demanding revenge—Is the Ghost his dead father seeking revenge, or is it the devil trying to lure Hamlet into sinful behavior?

■ Reading Strategies Worksheet

Compare and Contrast

The murder of Old Hamlet VERSUS the play, *The Mousetrap:* The setting of both the murder and the play is a garden where the king lies down to sleep. Both Old Hamlet and the actor "king" are killed by having poison poured into their ears. Just as Claudius sought to win Gertrude's affections following the murder of Old Hamlet, the actor "murderer" tries to woo the widowed queen in the pantomime that precedes the play. However, while Old Hamlet is murdered by his brother, the king in the play is murdered by his nephew.

Hamlet's opinion of his father VERSUS Hamlet's opinion of his mother: Hamlet respects and admires his father. In his outburst against his mother, Hamlet says that his father was noble, graceful, and godlike. Hamlet, however, upbraids his mother for her lustful, duplicitous, and corrupt behavior. He thinks she is hypocritical, weak, and fickle.

The murder of Old Hamlet VERSUS the murder of Polonius: The murder of Old Hamlet was planned and carried out by Claudius so that he could gain control of the throne. Hamlet is left to avenge his father's murder. Polonius, however, is accidentally murdered by Hamlet, who thought he was killing Claudius. Laertes is now responsible for avenging his father's death.

FOLLOW-UP: The comparison between Hamlet's friends tells something about the characters, revealing who is, and who is not, an ethical, honorable person. The comparison between Old Hamlet's murder and *The Mousetrap* advances the plot, because it helps

Hamlet decide on a course of action; it also sharpens the conflict between Hamlet and Claudius. Hamlet's conflicting opinions of his parents reveal not only Gertrude's and Old Hamlet's characters, but they also help convey Hamlet's anguish over his father's death and his mother's subsequent actions. Hamlet's outburst to his mother also reveals his conflict with her. Contrasting the murders of Old Hamlet and Polonius clarifies the conflict between Laertes and Hamlet. Both young men are seeking to right the wrongs done to their fathers. Contrasting these two murders shows that acts of revenge will be integral to the plot.

■ Test: Act III

A. *(20 points)*

1. a
2. b
3. d
4. b
5. a

B. *(50 points)*

6. Hamlet, still pretending to be mad, speaks cruelly to Ophelia, bursting into a tirade against women's lust and duplicity. He tells Ophelia that her best course would be to live out her life in a nunnery.

7. Ophelia is convinced that Hamlet is mad. Claudius is unsure, worrying that Hamlet's madness might be an act.

8. Hamlet speaks openly and forthrightly to Horatio, giving up his mad act. Clearly, Hamlet respects and trusts Horatio; he praises him as a true friend, in contrast to the court flatterers.

9. A Player Queen and Player King embrace. Then she leaves him as he goes to sleep on a bank of flowers. Another man enters, removes the Player King's crown, and pours poison into the sleeping king's ear. The murderer then woos the Player Queen with gifts.

10. Claudius plans to send Hamlet to England.

11. Hamlet does not want to kill Claudius while he is in a state of grace. He wants to kill him, as Claudius killed his father, in a way that will send the king's soul into purgatory.

12. Claudius learns that, as much as he would like to repent for his sins of murder and covetousness, he cannot.

13. Hamlet believes he is stabbing Claudius, but it turns out to be Polonius behind the curtain.

14. Polonius's tendency to be meddlesome puts him in the position that leads to his death.

15. Hamlet, as the accused murderer of Polonius, will likely lose the support of the people of Denmark as well as the support of the members of the court, thus securing Claudius' position.

C. *(30 points)*

Answers to these questions will vary. Individual answers should indicate the student's understanding of the events in Act III and the character's personalities and motivations. The best answers will be supported by examples or quotes from the play.

a. Answers should indicate an awareness that because Hamlet now knows for sure that Claudius murdered his father, the stage is set for actions that will avenge Old Hamlet's murder.

b. Answers should indicate knowledge that Hamlet regards death as a deliverance from the frustrations and woes of life; on the other hand, he muses on death as frightening and dreadful. He muses that it is only the fear of the unknown that keeps people like himself from committing suicide.

c. Answers should indicate an awareness of Claudius as a complex character. He is not simply an evil villain, but he is also a clever ruler and a man beset with regrets for the outcome of his actions.

d. Answers should indicate an awareness of the

moral dilemma Hamlet faces in seeking to avenge his father's death, which will, in turn, place him in the dangerous political position of murdering the king and his mother's husband.

Act IV

■ Making Meanings

> **READING CHECK**
>
> **a.** Claudius hesitates to "put the strong law" on Hamlet because the prince is extremely popular with the common people. Later, he also tells Laertes that he knows how much Hamlet means to Gertrude.
>
> **b.** Hamlet bitterly mocks Rosencrantz and Guildenstern, telling Rosencrantz that he is a "sponge" that soaks up the king's favor. Rosencrantz replies that he does not understand Hamlet, who then tells him, "I am glad of it; a knavish speech sleeps in a foolish ear."
>
> **c.** Hamlet resolves to delay no longer in taking his revenge. The sight of the Norwegian soldiers' bravery in risking death on the battlefield spurs Hamlet on to a new decisiveness.
>
> **d.** Ophelia sings a sad lament for the death of a "true-love." She also sings a ballad about a young lady betrayed by her lover. The garbled, incoherent nature of her songs suggests that she has slipped into insanity.
>
> **e.** Laertes becomes Claudius's new ally in the plot against Hamlet. Claudius asserts that Hamlet was responsible for Polonius's death, and that the mad prince also poses a threat to the king's own safety.
>
> **f.** Gertrude reports that Ophelia made fantastic garlands of flowers beside the brook. Then she climbed the willow tree to hang her coronet on one of its branches. The branch broke and Ophelia fell into the stream. She floated in the water, seemingly unconscious of any danger and singing songs and hymns. The weight of her wet clothes pulled her beneath the surface, and she drowned.

1. Responses will vary. Students should recognize that, even though revenge might be motivated by purposes of loyalty and honor, the resulting behavior on the part of these characters—specifically Hamlet and Laertes—might be described as disloyal and dishonorable or "two wrongs don't make a right." Ultimately, revenge is self-destructive.

2. Responses will vary. In general, students should point out that Hamlet's insults to the king in his mad scene (Scene 3) are pregnant with meaning, sometimes foreshadowing Claudius's death. Beneath his pretense of madness, Hamlet is menacing. Ophelia, on the other hand, displays a complete loss of sanity in her mad scene (Scene 5), mingling references to her father's death and Hamlet's rejection. The scenes reveal vulnerability in each character. Hamlet is vulnerable because he does not know the precise nature of the plots that the king may have set in motion against him. Ophelia's vulnerability is striking and pathetic; she has been cruelly manipulated by Claudius and Polonius, and Hamlet's rejection of her must have seemed harsh and inexplicable.

3. The political situation has changed in that Claudius now confronts a new threat; the angry Laertes, who has been swayed by the popular rumors that Claudius was responsible for Polonius's death. Claudius must now do his best to deflect Laertes's thirst for vengeance. He accomplishes this through a series of half-truths, persuading Laertes that Hamlet is the young man's true enemy.

4. In Scene 5, Horatio persuades Gertrude to see Ophelia; he is cautioned by Claudius to follow Ophelia closely—a job he seems to have forgotten. Horatio's only part in the action occurs in Scene 6, where he reads Hamlet's letter aloud. The letter advances the plot by revealing that Hamlet has escaped harm from the pirates; he has also foiled Claudius's plan to have him murdered in England. The letter also increases the audience's suspense with its announcement that Hamlet has

suddenly returned to Denmark. Perhaps Horatio's comparatively small role in the events of this act reflects the fact that Shakespeare portrays him primarily in dialogue with Hamlet as the paragon of a loyal friend. With Hamlet absent from the court for most of the act, there is no opportunity for such a characterization.

5. Students should point out that, in Hamlet's last major soliloquy, the hero condemns "thinking too precisely on the event" as an excuse for cowardice. Hamlet now realizes that honor demands action. The sight of the soldiers' courage in carrying out their vain military objective shames him; he reflects that he himself, with "a father killed, a mother stained," has far more obligation to risk his life than Fortinbras's men. Hamlet concludes by making up his mind to take his vengeance, no matter what the cost to his own safety.

6. A possible answer would apply Ophelia's statement as follows: Ophelia herself knew that she was being manipulated by the king and by her father, yet she did not suspect that madness would be the psychological cost of this manipulation; Hamlet has known the sorrow of his own predicament, but until late in Act IV he has not known how to resolve his doubts and uncertainties and to take action; Gertrude has known that her marriage to Claudius is corrupt, but she has not known until very recently (III, 4) that she could take action to ally herself with her son against the king.

7. A possible answer might include Hamlet's remarks about a "fat king," his talk about a king going "a progress through the guts of a beggar," his command to Claudius to seek Polonius's body in "the other place" (hell), and his ironic farewell to Claudius, addressing the king as "dear mother." If Hamlet were not supposedly insane, each of these remarks might be considered as treasonous or, at the least, disrespectful.

8. Among the problems that exist are Hamlet's unexplained whereabouts on Danish soil; what Hamlet will do when he arrives at court on the following day; whether or not the poisoning plot of Claudius and Laertes will succeed; whether Claudius will be able to continue to exploit Laertes's grief and rage for his own ends; how Hamlet will react if he learns of the death of Ophelia; and what role Gertrude will play in any confrontation between her husband and her son. Students will have various answers to describe how each of these problems might be resolved. Most students will sense that the conflict between Claudius and Hamlet is now too serious for the play to have a happy ending.

9. Responses will vary. For example, students might discuss how thinking too much about how to approach a homework assignment rather than addressing it when it is assigned can cause them to miss the assignment deadline and lose points as a result. Some students might cite social situations in which fear has kept them from acting directly, allowing problems to escalate in the mean time. Others might discuss situations in works of literature, in movies, or in a television series in which a character's resistance to decisive action results in a variety of problems.

10. Students might refer to familiar works of literature or to movies or television shows that are currently popular. Most students will recognize that characters who dedicate themselves to revenge rarely emerge happily as the plot is resolved.

■ Reading Strategies Worksheet

Determining Cause and Effect

CAUSE: Hamlet watches Fortinbras's troops marching to invade a town in Poland.

EFFECT: Hamlet, inspired by Fortinbras's sense of duty and determination, decides to move forward with his plans for revenge against Claudius.

CAUSE: Hamlet, while feigning insanity, rejects Ophelia. Later, Ophelia finds out that her father has been killed.

EFFECT: Ophelia goes insane.

CAUSE: Polonius is killed and news of his death reaches Laertes.

EFFECT: Laertes returns to Denmark from France.

CAUSE: Hamlet's ship is attacked by pirates on its voyage to England.

EFFECT: Hamlet returns to Denmark.

CAUSE: Laertes learns that Hamlet killed Polonius.

EFFECT: Laertes agrees to help Claudius in a plot to kill Hamlet.

FOLLOW-UP: Responses will vary. Most students will recognize that the final act will include a confrontation between Hamlet and Laertes or between Hamlet and Claudius (or both). Hamlet has made a decision to take action against his father's murderer, and Claudius and Laertes have made plans to kill Hamlet. Most students will recognize that because this is a tragedy, some or all of these characters will die.

■ Test: Act IV

A. *(20 points)*

1. b
2. c
3. a
4. b
5. c

B. *(50 points)*

6. Hamlet has left the corpse in the lobby.

7. Claudius has planned for Hamlet to be killed.

8. The army is headed for Poland, where they engage in what seems to be a futile fight for territory.

9. On his return, Laertes accuses Claudius of being responsible for Polonius's death. Claudius responds calmly, saying that he will reveal to

Laertes the identity of the murderer.

10. Ophelia sings pathetic songs with garbled and incoherent lyrics. She seems to be unsure of her surroundings. She scatters flowers about, as if on a coffin or in a graveyard.

11. Laertes is popular with the people, and many have been calling for Claudius's overthrow so that Laertes can become king.

12. Hamlet tells Horatio that following his ship's departure for England, it was attacked by pirates. During the fight, Hamlet boarded the pirate ship, becoming the pirate's sole prisoner. He assures Horatio that the pirates treated him well and hints that he has returned to Denmark. He asks Horatio to hasten to meet him.

13. Claudius tells Laertes that Hamlet killed Polonius and is plotting to kill Claudius. He says that he could not punish Hamlet because Hamlet is so popular with the people and because Gertrude loves him so dearly.

14. Claudius plans to stage a dueling match between Laertes and Hamlet. Laertes will use a foil that has been dipped in poison. As a back-up plan, Claudius will offer Hamlet a goblet of poisoned wine to drink.

15. Mad and distracted, Ophelia falls into a brook and floats until the weight of her wet clothes pulls her under, and she drowns.

C. *(30 points)*

Answers to these questions will vary. Individual answers should indicate the student's understanding of the events in Act IV and the character's personalities and motivations. The best answers will be supported by examples or quotes from the play.

a. Answers should indicate students' awareness that Claudius did not want to rock the political boat. By holding a large, state funeral, which would be expected in such a case, attention would be drawn to the personal turmoil in the court. He wanted to avoid at all costs having issues of his guilt in Old Hamlet's murder raised.

b. Answers should indicate knowledge that Hamlet's shame is linked to his inability to act. He is motivated to consider his shortcoming when he talks to Fortinbras's captain, who describes the unnecessary mission he and his troops are on to win back land from Poland.

c. Answers should indicate awareness of the following: Hamlet reacted to knowledge of the circumstances of his father's death by questioning them. He falls into depression and despair and agonizes over whether the Ghost is really that of his father or, perhaps, the devil. Laertes acts forthrightly with anger, eager to lash out at anyone who might be responsible for his father's death.

d. Answers should be supported with examples of quotations from the text. Students may note that Gertrude, far from demonstrating frailty, has remained quite strong during Hamlet's ordeal.

Answer Key (cont.)

The Tragedy of Hamlet

Act V

■ Making Meanings

READING CHECK

a. The Gravediggers talk about the upcoming funeral of Ophelia as they go about their work. They debate whether Ophelia, as a presumed suicide, can be buried in consecrated ground in the cemetery. The Gravediggers also trade black-humor jokes about various professions.

b. As a presumed suicide, Ophelia is considered by the church to have committed the unpardonable sin of despair. She is thus denied the full burial rites.

c. Yorick was the jester at the court of Old Hamlet. Hamlet says that, as a child, he knew "poor Yorick" well and he speaks of him with fond remembrance.

d. While on shipboard, Hamlet found in Rosencrantz's and Guildenstern's papers a letter from Claudius ordering Hamlet's execution in England. Hamlet substituted another commission, commanding the deaths of Rosencrantz and Guildenstern. He sealed the new commission with the signet ring of Old Hamlet.

e. Claudius's plan involves two parts, both revolving around a fencing match to be staged between Hamlet and Laertes as an athletic exhibition, complete with wagers on the winner. Relying on Laertes' skill as a swordsman and on Hamlet's trusting nature, Claudius will arrange for Laertes' foil to be dipped in poison. Should the foil so much as scratch Hamlet's skin, the prince will die. As a back-up plan, Claudius tells Laertes that he will have a poisoned cup of wine offered to Hamlet when the prince calls for a drink to quench his thirst.

1. Responses will vary. Sample answers might include "Death of the Danish Royals" or "Flights of Angels Sing Thee to Thy Rest" (taken from the text).

2. A possible answer would be that the black humor and graphic detail result in a grotesque tone that mingles humor, disgust, and pathos.

3. Some students will say that this speech to

Horatio reveals Hamlet's new acceptance of the mysterious action of providence: He trusts now in a "divinity that shapes our ends." In contrast to his former caution, he now emphasizes that indiscretion can sometimes serve people well especially when the most carefully laid plans fail.

4. Hamlet reveals that he is now sorry that he forgot himself with Laertes. He feels that Laertes, determined to avenge his slain father, has something in common with himself.

5. A possible answer would point out that in his remarks about Yorick, Hamlet muses on mortality and the disintegration of the body as the common destiny of humanity—as true for Yorick as for Alexander the Great and Julius Caesar. Later, just before the duel, Hamlet's sense of resignation seems to have acquired a religious dimension. He tells Horatio not to be concerned about the outcome of the duel because God has fixed the time for every person's death. The important consideration now, according to Hamlet, is not the hour of his death but his readiness to meet it at any hour.

6. After Gertrude drinks from the poisoned cup, she reveals to Hamlet with her dying breath that the wine was poisoned. Most students will probably agree that this is her final way of helping her son in his struggle against Claudius.

7. A possible answer explaining the absence of soliloquies in the final act is that Hamlet has at last resolved his doubts about the truth of the Ghost's claim that Claudius murdered Old Hamlet; he may also have come to terms with his own guilt, shame, and fears of mortality. He confides his thoughts in Horatio.

8. Fortinbras's election as the new head of government is ironic because it represents a sharp reversal from the situation in Act I. At the opening of the play we learn that Fortinbras was an ambitious youth, raising armies to recover the lands that had been lost to Old Hamlet. Student descriptions of the report that Horatio will give to Fortinbras will differ. In general, however, students should point out the irony of Claudius's treachery and his disguise of himself as a legitimate ruler; the irony of Hamlet's betrayal by his friends, Rosencrantz and Guildenstern; the irony of the outstandingly intelligent and sensitive Hamlet having to feign madness to find out the truth about his father's murder; the irony in the chance death of the meddlesome Polonius; the ironies involved in the failure of Claudius's plot, resulting in his own death and that of Gertrude; and the final irony of Hamlet's death at the hands of Laertes, a man with whom he had much in common.

9. Responses will vary. Some students will find the many deaths disturbing. At the same time, they will most likely recognize that any other outcome would have left unresolved problems.

10. Most students will agree with Lewis's statement, noting that Hamlet is a tragedy in which most of the leading characters die. More specifically, readers or audience members are continuously reminded of death throughout the play—issues of murder, the soul's destiny, burial rites, and so forth keep death the play's central concern.

■ Reading Strategies Worksheet

Organizing Information

Gertrude dies from unknowingly drinking the poisoned wine meant for Hamlet.

Hamlet dies from being wounded by Laertes's poisoned sword.

Horatio lives and will tell the story of murder and revenge that has just ended with multiple deaths.

Claudius dies. He is mortally wounded when Hamlet strikes him with the poisoned sword; Hamlet also makes him drink the poisoned wine.

Laertes dies after Hamlet wounds him with the poisoned sword.

Fortinbras lives and will become king of Denmark. Horatio and Fortinbras are alive at the end of the play.

FOLLOW-UP: Some students will support Shakespeare's ending, saying that, given all the foul deeds that occurred in the play, everyone was doomed to die. Others may agree that Claudius should die because he should be punished for his ignoble deeds, but students might suggest that Hamlet and Laertes be saved because they did not really do anything wrong (although some might think Hamlet should be punished for killing Polonius). Most students will probably know, however, that even if Hamlet's crimes were excusable, he is destined to die because he is the protagonist in the tragedy. Students will probably agree that Horatio, who has remained above the fray, stayed honest and loyal to his friend, and been privy to all the clandestine activities, is the logical character to tell the tale. Some students might question the appearance of Fortinbras as a clumsy device used to hasten the end of the play. Others, however, might support Shakespeare's decision to give Denmark to the young Norwegian because he has been presented as Hamlet's more active, aggressive counterpart throughout the play.

■ Test: Act V

A. *(20 points)*

1. b
2. c
3. b
4. c
5. b

B. *(50 points)*

6. Some people suspect that Ophelia might have committed suicide, which is considered a mortal sin by the church. In cases of suicide, the person is denied full burial rites.

7. Hamlet's behavior serves to further antagonize Laertes, firming up Claudius's plan to have Laertes kill Hamlet in a duel.

8. Hamlet replaced the letter ordering his own death with one ordering that Rosencrantz and Guildenstern be killed. He sealed the letter using his father's signet ring.

9. She asks that Hamlet treat Laertes with courtesy.

10. The king wagers six Barbary horses, against which Laertes wagers six French rapiers and poniards and three "carriages" or hangers.

11. Claudius first offers Hamlet the poisoned cup after Hamlet scores the first hit.

12. Laertes dies because, after a scramble, the foils are exchanged and Hamlet wounds him with the poisoned tip. Gertrude drinks from the poisoned cup and dies. After the dying Laertes tells Hamlet, who is also wounded with the poisoned tip, what has happened, Hamlet stabs Claudius with the poisoned foil and forces him to drink from the poisoned cup.

13. Hamlet tells Horatio to live on and to clear Hamlet's name by reporting "my cause aright / To the unsatisfied."

14. They bring the news that Rosencrantz and Guildenstern are dead.

15. The "illness" in Denmark was a reflection of the corruption in government and the corruption in the private lives of the rulers. After the court is purged by the deaths of Claudius, Gertrude, Hamlet, Laertes, Polonius, and Ophelia, as well as Rosencrantz and Guildenstern, the country is ready to heal itself under the leadership of Fortinbras.

C. *(30 points)*

a. Answers should include a description of the graveyard scene and the gravediggers. Most students will realize that Shakespeare is offering a bit of comic relief from the unrelenting drama of the play to this point, particularly considering what is about to occur in the conclusion of the act.

b. Opinions should be supported by references to specific events or by direct quotations from the

characters. Students should recognize that, with Gertrude's death, Hamlet's dilemma about killing his mother's husband is removed, and the way is cleared for Claudius's death.

c. Answers should include several of the following variations on the themes of love and loyalty: (1) Hamlet's initial love and subsequent rejection of Ophelia; (2) Ophelia's divided loyalties between Hamlet and her father; (3) Horatio's undivided loyalty to Hamlet; (4) Gertrude's corrupted loyalty to her husband and then her courageous loyalty to Hamlet toward the play's end; (5) Hamlet's loyalty to his father and his ambivalent feelings toward his mother; (6) Claudius's respect for Gertrude's love of her son, as contrasted with his betrayal of his own brother.

d. Answers should be fully supported with reasons.

Literary Elements Worksheets

■ Conflict

Hamlet and Claudius: External. Initially, Hamlet's conflict with Claudius is that Claudius, who is Old Hamlet's brother, married Hamlet's mother soon after her husband's death. Hamlet thinks the marriage is decadent and inappropriate. The conflict escalates when Hamlet learns from the Ghost that Claudius murdered Old Hamlet.

Hamlet and Gertrude: External. Hamlet is angry and disappointed in his mother because she remarried so quickly. Her marriage to her brother-in-law would have been characterized as incestuous. Hamlet agonizes over Gertrude's behavior, which he considers lustful and immoral.

Hamlet and Hamlet: Internal. Hamlet struggles with his melancholy disposition and his tendency to think rather than act. After he realizes that he must avenge his father's murder by killing Claudius, he vacillates between thinking about what he should do and initiating a plan for revenge.

FOLLOW-UP: Some students might say that Hamlet will have more trouble overcoming his external conflicts because he cannot control the behavior or actions of Gertrude and Claudius, although he can control or change his own behavior. Others might suggest, however, that Hamlet's internal conflicts will be harder to overcome. He puts enormous pressure on himself, because he knows he must conquer his personal battles before he can confront his adversaries.

■ Theme

Rosencrantz and Guildenstern with Hamlet
APPEARANCE: Rosencrantz and Guildenstern are Hamlet's good friends, who have come to Denmark out of concern for the distraught prince.

REALITY: They are hypocrites who have agreed to align themselves with Claudius by spying on Hamlet.

Claudius and Gertrude speak to Rosencrantz and Guildenstern about Hamlet
APPEARANCE: Claudius and Gertrude are Hamlet's concerned parents, who have summoned his old friends (Rosencrantz and Guildenstern) in an attempt to lift his spirits.

REALITY: Claudius and Gertrude direct Rosencrantz and Guildenstern to spy on Hamlet to learn the cause of his behavior.

Hamlet with Ophelia
APPEARANCE: Ophelia reports that Hamlet was wild, disheveled, and erratic when he came to see her in her sitting room.

REALITY: Hamlet is continuing his mad pose, knowing that Ophelia will report his violent behavior to her father, who will report it to Claudius.

FOLLOW-UP: Responses will vary. By pretending to be something they are not—Claudius, the concerned uncle, and Hamlet, the crazy prince—both characters become actors. Hamlet's purpose in behaving dishonestly is to discover the truth about his father's murder, which could be construed as dishonest behavior with a positive motive. Some of his acting is neutral, rather than positive or negative. His exchanges with Polonius, for example, are relatively harmless, and Hamlet seems to enjoy making fun of the old man while effecting his mad persona. He also knows Polonius will report his "insane" behavior to Claudius, which is what Hamlet wants. Claudius will be less suspicious of Hamlet if he thinks his nephew is out of touch with reality. Claudius, however, seems to be the more dangerous actor because he acts to conceal a base crime and to plot further violence. Claudius embodies the negative powers of the hypocrite: He pretends to be good and benevolent, but he is really the assassin underneath.

■ Irony

Irony: Hamlet and the audience know that Claudius's soul is anything but free, and that the events in *The Mousetrap* are meant to touch Claudius directly by forcing him to reveal his guilt. Claudius does not realize he is being tested.

Irony: Looking at the situation carefully, Hamlet realises that murdering Claudius while he is praying would have the ironic effect of sending his soul to heaven, which is a courtesy Claudius did not grant Old Hamlet (who was murdered before he could repent his sins). Hamlet does not want to cheat his father of the fullest revenge on Claudius.

Irony: With these lines, Claudius reveals that Hamlet's delay was needless because Claudius has found himself unable to repent. Hamlet does not realize that he has just spared the king's life for nothing, but the audience can see the irony in Claudius's words and Hamlet's procrastination.

FOLLOW-UP: Dramatic irony gives the audience "behind the scenes" information and makes them, at times, omniscient observers. When readers and spectators understand dramatic irony, they can gain insight into characters' motives, which often affect plot development. Sometimes, irony can help the audience anticipate events and predict characters' actions.

■ Imagery

HEARING

Example: "Her brother is in secret come from France; / Feeds on his wonder, keeps himself in clouds, / And wants not buzzers to infect his ear / With pestilent speeches of his father's death, . . ." (Act IV, Scene 5, lines 88–91). Claudius compares the reports Laertes hears about Polonius's death, which poison the young man with grief and rage, to buzzing insects that can infect a body with pestilence and disease.

TOUCH

Example: "O heat, dry up my brains! Tears seven times salt / Burn out the sense and virtue of mine eye!" (Act IV, Scene 5, lines 154–155). Laertes comments on the relief he would experience if his emotions and tears would completely dry up, which would spare him from feeling his grief. The image is created through the language of touch: His brain will "dry up," the salt from his tears will "burn out" his eyes and his tormented consciousness.

TASTE

Example: "But, like the owner of a foul disease, / To keep it from divulging, let it feed / Even on the pith of life" (Act IV, Scene 1, lines 21–23). Claudius has kept Hamlet's "madness" a secret, which has caused it to feed on itself and intensify, much like a disease will feed on and spread throughout its host body. Shakespeare uses the language of tainted consumption to create an image of rot and decay.

SMELL

Example: "But indeed, if you find him not within this month, you shall nose him as you go up the stairs into the lobby" (Act IV, Scene 3, lines 36–38). Hamlet creates an image of smell as he indicates where Polonius's dead body is stashed. The audience should understand that Hamlet is saying the corpse will begin to stink if it is not found soon.

FOLLOW-UP: The recurrent theme of disease, decay, and corruption is reflected in most of these images. As the Danish court becomes more treacherous, characters increasingly give in to behavior that is character-ized through this tormented and troubling imagery.

■ Plot

1. Events leading up to dramatic climax:

The animosity Laertes feels toward Hamlet is exacerbated when Hamlet follows Laertes into Ophelia's grave. The two fight and must be separated. Laertes and Hamlet eventually face each other in a fencing contest—a match that is, in fact, a trap set by Laertes and Claudius for Hamlet. Laertes prepares to duel with a poisoned foil, and Claudius, a spectator along with Gertrude, Horatio, and others, has prepared a poisoned cup of wine to offer Hamlet during the match.

2. Dramatic climax:

After Laertes and Hamlet are both mortally wounded and Gertrude drinks from the poisoned cup meant for Hamlet, Laertes reveals the secret of the sabotaged foil. Hamlet then stabs Claudius with the poisoned weapon and also forces his uncle to drink from the tainted cup that killed Gertrude. The dramatic climax occurs when Hamlet discharges his obligation to his father's ghost by killing Claudius.

3. Resolution:

Fortinbras, who will become king of Denmark, orders a military funeral for Hamlet. The conflict between Norway and Denmark is settled with the Norwegian's assumption of the throne and reclamation of his lands. Horatio, the scholar, will become the narrator, as he tells the tale of intrigue, revenge, and murder that has consumed the Danish court. Hamlet's troubled soul presumably rests in peace.

FOLLOW-UP: Hamlet finally takes action in the fifth act. In the first four acts of the play, Hamlet was philosophically committed to seeking revenge on Claudius, but the young prince's plans remained unrealized as he seemed to think more and act less. In Act V, however, Hamlet is no longer concerned about dying. He seems at peace with his destiny and confident in his identity as the one who will right the wrong done to his father.

Exploring the Connections

■ Just Lather, That's All

> **READING CHECK**
>
> **a.** Captain Torres comes into the shop for a shave.
>
> **b.** Captain Torres's beard is thick because he has been searching for rebels for four days and has not had time to shave.
>
> **c.** The barber keeps his status as a rebel quiet so he can be a more effective informant.
>
> **d.** Captain Torres hanged and mutilated the rebels in the town.

1. Responses will vary. Students may feel that political beliefs justify killing, or that killing (even if condoned by war or warlike circumstances) is never right.

2. The barber is struggling with the images of himself as a hero and as a murderer.

3. The details of the political conflict are probably not revealed because the story is not concerned with which side is right but about the barber's internal conflict over committing murder. It is important that the audience sees that the barber thinks his side is right, but it is not important that the audience agree with him.

Connecting with the Play

The barber is certain that Torres is guilty; Hamlet has doubts until he sees Claudius react to *The Mousetrap*. The barber's quarrel with Torres is almost entirely political, whereas Hamlet's quarrel with Claudius is political and personal. The barber fantasizes about being a hero if he kills Torres; Hamlet does not have such fantasies. Hamlet might agree with the barber's thought that "No one deserves to have someone else make the sacrifice of becoming a murderer."

■ Plays and Performances

> **READING CHECK**
>
> **a.** All kinds of people, from tailors to earls, went to the theater in Shakespeare's time.
>
> **b.** A performance of *Richard the Second* was banned from the stage because it shows Richard renouncing his crown and counselors feared it might incite rebellion.
>
> **c.** Clergymen discouraged people from attending the theater because they feared that the theater encouraged idleness and immorality.
>
> **d.** A trumpeter would sound three calls on his trumpet to announce that they were ready to perform.

1. Responses will vary. Students might note the excitement of live performance, the diversion of the spectacle, and the scarcity of other forms of entertainment.

2. As the plays were only rarely rehearsed with the entire company, the actors would be reacting to each other for the first time. The performances were probably both more spontaneous and somewhat rougher than modern stage plays.

3. Responses will vary. Students should mention that the physical closeness of the audience to the players would encourage more audience participation. And at each enactment of a play actors would re-interpret their roles, thus keeping the audience off balance.

Connecting with the Play

Responses will vary but should draw on the information in Brown's essay as well as the play. Some students might note that watching the play in such a busy, distracting environment might lighten the tone. Others might point out that, because going to the theater was considered a mildly subversive activity, the audience might be especially aware of the play's political implications. Some will undoubtedly contend that, given the circumstances of its original production, we should not take the play so seriously.

■ In a Dark Time

> **READING CHECK**
>
> **a.** The speaker meets himself, or, more precisely, his shadow.
>
> **b.** "Midnight comes again," that is, a darkness of spirit is not confined to night.
>
> **c.** He says, "I know the purity of pure despair."

1. Responses will vary. Students are likely to have difficulty understanding this poem and should be encouraged to explore its images and emotion as a means to interpretation.

2. The poet uses the metaphor of searching for his shadow on a dark night to describe his internal search for his whole self.

3. Not understanding if he sees a cave or a path is symbolic of the poet's internal struggle. The cave suggests the end point of a journey. It is an enclosed space, which is to say, metaphorically, potentially safe, but also a dead end. The winding path means a continued struggle but also, potentially, a directed way towards peace.

4. Responses will vary. Some students will see the declaration of God entering the mind and the poet's assertion that "one is One" as a clear restoration of peace and thus a resolution. Others may focus on the final phrase, "free in the tearing wind," as an avowal that no resolution is readily available; peace will continue to alternate with madness.

Connecting with the Play

Both questions are asked out of despair, and each engages the issue of whether absolute values or attitudes are more "noble" than adapting to circumstances. Roethke suggests that it is changing circumstances that make a stable, noble mind seem mad. The implication is that one ought to cling to one's own sense of spirit regardless of what happens around one. Hamlet makes similar inquiries but comes to different conclusions. He has no doubt that his own ideas about loyalty and love are superior to his mother's, but he

wonders if he should live to suffer the consequences of her bad judgment. (In other words, in this soliloquy, he does not doubt his own sanity; he only doubts how he should respond to "outrageous fortune.") Hamlet decides that it is better to endure the pains of life than to risk the possibly greater pains that may come after death; however, he does not believe this to be the nobler path, insofar as he says, "Thus conscience does make cowards of us all."

■ Raymond Chandler's *Hamlet*

> **READING CHECK**
>
> **a.** Horatio narrates this short story.
>
> **b.** Ophelia is described as Hamlet's "main squeeze."
>
> **c.** The narrator says that Claudius "freaked" in reaction to the play within the play.
>
> **d.** Horatio is left wondering where his next paycheck will come from.

1. Responses will vary. Students may enjoy the parody of a hard-boiled detective story; other students may dislike trivializing a serious and classic tragedy.

2. The narrator uses this phrase to describe Claudius pouring poison in the king's ear.

3. The tone of this piece—created by applying a hard-boiled detective's perspective to a Shakespearean tragedy—is satirical and humorous.

Connecting with the Play

Responses to this creative exercise will vary.

■ *from* John Gielgud Directs Richard Burton in *Hamlet:* Journal of Rehearsals

> **READING CHECK**
>
> **a.** Gielgud proposes acting the play with minimal costumes, lighting, and scenery because he thinks the technical trappings distract and restrict both the actors and the audience.
>
> **b.** Richard Burton plays Hamlet in this production.
>
> **c.** Sir John Gielgud plays the Ghost in this production.

1. Responses will vary. Students may feel that traditional costumes are necessary for realism; other students may prefer costumes or non-costumes that enable the audience to imagine the play in virtually any time and place.

2. The minimal costumes and props, as well as Gielgud's apparent openness to cutting lines, support the reviewer's description of the production as "streamlined."

3. Responses will vary, but students should focus on the concrete details offered by the various reviews. The first reviewer gives precise detail to support his judgment of the production as "naked" and "bared down," but only vague superlatives to evaluate Burton's performance. The only concrete details the second reviewer offers are about the "bare platforms" and "high brick backing." The third reviewer supplies descriptive details of what he regards as Burton's poor performance, but none for the sets or costumes.

4. Responses will vary.

Connecting with the Play
Responses to this creative exercise will vary.

■ Two Poems by Maya Angelou

> **READING CHECK**
> a. Angelou compares her wiles to wounded pride.
> b. No, the insomniac does not manage to sleep.
> c. The speaker's tongue would be salty if she lets her tears flow into her mouth.
> d. The poem ends with the question "Will you have the grace to mourn for me?"*

1. Responses will vary. Students might mention sympathy, regret, and sadness.

2. Sleep is personified, and "plays coy, / aloof and disdainful."* Students might mention that the lines of "Insomniac" seem to drone, and the lines of "Mourning Grace" seem to hesitate.

*From "Mourning Grace" from *The Complete Collected Poems of Maya Angelou.* Copyright © 1994 by Maya Angelou. Reprinted by permission of **Gerald W. Purcell Associates, Ltd.**

3. Responses will vary, but they should be responsive to the pacing of the respective poems.

Connecting with the Play
Responses will vary but should be restricted to characters who seem to be, or have reason to be, suicidal at some point in the play. Many students will choose Ophelia because the poem resonates with her disappointed expectations and her tendency to focus on other people. Some students may choose Hamlet because of his open contemplation of suicide and because of his penchant for recitation.

■ The Olivier *Hamlet*

> **READING CHECK**
> a. Crowther means that in most stage presentations the audience cannot adequately see the action.
> b. Lawrence Oliver plays Hamlet.
> c. Olivier's Hamlet was different from any previous production of the play because it was on film.
> d. Crowther thinks Olivier's extensive editing makes the play easier to understand.

1. Hamlet's first soliloquy is much more concerned with Gertrude's remarriage than his father's death. Similarly, in Act III, scene 4, Hamlet focuses most of his rude address to his mother on her relationship with Claudius.

2. Responses will vary but should rely on specific examples from the play for support. Some students may argue that Rosencrantz and Guildenstern add too many distractions to an already complicated play. Others may point out that their presence contributes to the plot development, as a means for Hamlet to discover that Claudius is watching him. They may also note that in watching Hamlet's interactions with, and betrayal by, his childhood friends we have an additional opportunity to evaluate his character.

3. Responses will vary. Students may note that Hamlet must be presented as a believable lover of Ophelia and a plausible leader of his nation.

Answer Key *(cont.)*

The Tragedy of Hamlet

Connecting with the Play

Responses will vary.

■ Fear No More the Heat o' the Sun

> **READING CHECK**
>
> **a.** This song appears in Shakespeare's *Cymbeline*.
>
> **b.** Guiderius and Arviragus sing it to honor Fidele / Imogen.
>
> **c.** They think Fidele is dead.

1. Responses will vary. Students might mention the theme of inevitable death, the image of the chimney sweepers, or the image of the storm of life—the lightening and thunder—that need no longer be feared.

2. The superficial difference between "golden" children and soot-covered chimney sweepers reinforces the pathos of their shared fate: to come to dust.

3. The song occurs after Fidele is thought irrevocably dead, so it is more a song of consolation than consideration. Hamlet, however, is considering action and thus wants to think about both sides of the question. He shares the conclusion that death is an escape from pain but also fears unknown pains that may come after death. He, therefore, decides to live.

Connecting with the Play

Responses to this creative exercise will vary.

■ The Gibson *Hamlet*

> **READING CHECK**
>
> **a.** Ebert mentions *Romeo and Juliet*.
>
> **b.** The scene added is a wake for Hamlet's father.
>
> **c.** Ebert thinks that the actresses who play Gertrude and Ophelia are well cast.
>
> **d.** Yes, Ebert thinks the production intelligent and robust.

1. Responses will vary. Students may mention that, if Hamlet at least begins "upbeat," his tragedy is all the greater.

2. Ebert describes a Hamlet that is motivated by real world, mundane events. The physicality of the set reinforces this interpretation of a less cerebral Hamlet.

3. In marrying, both Claudius and Gertrude gain a more secure hold on the throne.

4. It encourages an interpretation of Ophelia as isolated and bereft.

Connecting with the Play

Responses will vary. Some students will feel that Gibson's status as a star and his robust acting will add to their appreciation of Hamlet, making the Dane seem more modern and real. Others may feel that Gibson detracts from what they perceive should be the character of Hamlet.

■ The Branagh *Hamlet*

> **READING CHECK**
>
> **a.** Positioning Hamlet in the foreground makes Hamlet's experience of the wedding the focus of the scene.
>
> **b.** Branagh's production was the first filmed version of the uncut play.
>
> **c.** Branagh sets the play in the nineteenth century.
>
> **d.** Ebert thinks the uncut version makes the reaction of Claudius more understandable.

1. Responses will vary. Students may note that understanding why a person does something evil adds immeasurably to the depth of characterization.

2. Gielgud and Olivier were most interested in emphasizing the play's language and psychology, and found scenery and props distracting. Zeffirelli and Branagh were much more interested in the play's physical presence and believability, and they found substantial sets more realistic.

Answer Key (cont.) The Tragedy of Hamlet

3. Seeing Polonius as foolish suggests that Claudius is likewise foolish for employing him as an advisor. It also shapes how we see the relationship among Ophelia, Laertes, and Polonius; a foolish Polonius often leads to an eye-rolling Ophelia and an impatient Laertes. Our reaction to Hamlet's taunting of Polonius is also shaped by how we read that character. A foolish Polonius makes Hamlet's taunts perhaps more humorous but certainly less clever.

4. Responses will vary. Students may note that a single interpretation that answers all questions is an impossibility that could never be created anyway.

Connecting with the Play
Responses to this creative exercise will vary.

■ Sonnet 146

READING CHECK
a. "[T]he center of my sinful earth" is the speaker's "Poor soul."
b. The general idea of the questions the sonnet asks is why spend time and energy on the passing fancies of life?
c. Worms, after death, will "Eat up thy charge."

1. Responses will vary. Students may mention outward artificial decoration and devouring worms.

2. The mansion is one's body and the lease one's life span. The servant is the body and the master is the soul.

3. The second part of the sonnet develops the idea that one should feed the soul at the body's expense.

4. It more closely resembles Hamlet's attitude in Act V, Scene 2, where he seems reconciled to death.

Connecting with the Play
Responses to this creative exercise will vary.

■ Test

■ Part I: Objective Questions *(30 points)*

1. F	**6.** c	**11.** c
2. T	**7.** a	**12.** d
3. T	**8.** d	**13.** a
4. F	**9.** c	**14.** b
5. T	**10.** b	**15.** c

■ Part II: Short-Answer Questions *(40 points)*

16. The mood is dark and ominous. The midnight setting and the talk of warfare and the supernatural help to establish the mood.

17. Hamlet is despairing and weary of the world. He is particularly distressed over his mother's hasty remarriage to Claudius. He condemns his mother and Claudius for their moral weakness.

18. After Hamlet meets the players, he asks them to perform a play of his choosing. The play includes a scene which closely resembles the murder of Old Hamlet as described by the Ghost. Hamlet hopes to determine by Claudius's reaction whether or not he actually performed the murder.

19. Responses may vary but should include the fact that Polonius seems shallow, sycophantic, and meddlesome. His interactions with his children and with Claudius lead to this conclusion.

20. After the murder scene, Claudius abruptly leaves the room. Hamlet surmises from this behavior that Claudius is guilty of murdering Old Hamlet.

21. Hamlet does not want to kill Claudius while he is in a state of grace. He wants to kill him, as Claudius killed his father, in a way that will send the king's soul to eternal damnation.

22. Hamlet, as the accused murderer of Polonius, will likely lose the support of the people of Denmark as well as the support of the members of the court.

150 The Tragedy of Hamlet

Copyright © by Holt, Rinehart and Winston. All rights reserved.

Answer Key *(cont.)*   *The Tragedy of Hamlet*

23. Ophelia sings pathetic songs with garbled and incoherent lyrics. She seems to be unsure of her surroundings. She scatters flowers about, as if on a coffin or in a graveyard.

24. The people call out for Laertes to become the new king. Claudius, of course, is threatened by this proposal and tries to draw Laertes into allegiance with him.

25. The "illness" in Denmark was a reflection of the corruption in government and the corruption in the private lives of the rulers. After the court is purged by the deaths of Claudius, Gertrude, Hamlet, Laertes, Polonius, and Ophelia, as well as Rosencrantz and Guildenstern, the country was ready to heal itself under the leadership of Fortinbras.

■ PART III: ESSAY QUESTIONS *(30 points)*

a. The jokes and puns and the parodies on the practice of law and religious rites provide comic relief at the same time as they reflect on the incongruities of life at Elsinore. They provide a comment from the common people on the actions of the upper classes and the conditions created by Claudius. In the dialogue of the gravedigger and Hamlet, with Hamlet as straight man, Shakespeare highlights more of the equivocation—of people not giving straight answers, not speaking truly—which has characterized a good deal of the action of the play. We are reminded of what life and death have been reduced to in the reign of Claudius. In the scene following Polonius's death, Hamlet speaks to the king precisely the way the gravedigger now speaks to him. Humor and irony thus unite the "high" and "low" worlds of the play.

b. The first soliloquy outlines Hamlet's feelings about the recent happenings in his family, the fact that he is quite alone and despairing, with no one to talk to. More than half the speech focuses on the actions of his mother. In the second soliloquy, following the audition of the players, Hamlet berates himself for his inaction, while the actor, who is "only acting," gets worked up in the tragedy he portrays. Hamlet plans to use the actors to present "something like the murder of [his] father / Before [his] uncle /" to "catch the conscience of the king" and let it draw forth the guilt of Claudius so that he all but confesses publicly to the crime. In the last soliloquy after failing to act, Hamlet falls to self-deprecation again. However, this time, after encountering the forces of Fortinbras, a "real" person, not an actor, acting forthrightly and passionately, he vows finally to do the same.

c. Student responses will vary; all should include descriptive references to Hamlet's relationships and attitudes toward Ophelia and Gertrude and some attempt at an analytical discussion as to *why* Hamlet acts the way he does toward each woman. In some discussions, there may be references to the workings of the Oedipus complex and Hamlet's extremely emotional attachment to his mother. Students may also note that Hamlet generalizes about *all* women based on his mother's actions.

d. Responses will vary but students should see in the fragmented speech of each woman the moral and psychological sources of her breakdown, beyond the particular events referred to by each character. Both refer to their fathers, and to death; where Ophelia speaks of love, thwarted or disappointed, Lady Macbeth speaks more of the blood that will not wash away, the crime that lives on no matter what.

e. Polonius represents a variation on the theme of fathers and children, affecting Hamlet through the advice he gives Ophelia and through the kind of entrapment he imagines will cause Hamlet to reveal his motives; also, his accidental death at the hands of Hamlet offers another variation on the theme of revenge, with Laertes moving to avenge his father's death, and becoming in the process another pawn used by Claudius to advance his own ends.

Rosencrantz and Guildenstern represent the breakdown of friendship and traditional loyalties in Claudius's Denmark; they were boyhood friends of Hamlet who are too eager to go where the power is and accordingly become pawns of Claudius in his power struggle with Hamlet.

Horatio is one of the few honest people we see, perhaps the only one Hamlet can speak to. (This is one reason we see so little of him.) He represents balance, truth, and integrity in a world false and conflicted. Fortinbras adds more of the political theme as well as being another of the sons out to gain revenge for a father's death. His march through Denmark is a turning-point in Hamlet's "blunted purpose" to avenge Old Hamlet's death. If Laertes is predominantly impulsive and Hamlet meditative, Fortinbras seems more of a balance between these two attitudes.

f. Responses will vary but should be supported with references to both *Hamlet* and the **Connection.**

Notes

Notes

The Tragedy of Hamlet